**Dairyless Milks . . . Creams . . . And Ice Cream
Sugarless Sweets And Desserts
A Magic Mix For Instant Baking
Soups . . . Sauces . . . Main Dishes . . . Snacks**

Made from natural, wholesome foods—
and prepared in only a few minutes in your
blender.

This is what this marvelous **two-in-one**
cookbook is all about, combining all the delicious recipes contained in Frieda Nusz's two
best-selling cookbooks, **Wheat And Sugar-
Free** and **Blenderbusz.**

If you've thought that "health foods" can't
taste marvelous—or that a blender is too
hard to use in your kitchen—let Frieda Nusz
show you the way to new and better nutrition,
taste and ease in your cooking.

THE NATURAL FOODS
BLENDER
COOKBOOK

FRIEDA H. NUSZ

Keats Publishing, Inc. New Canaan, Connecticut

Pivot edition published 1972

Copyright © 1966, 1968 and 1972
by Frieda H. Nusz

All Rights Reserved

Printed in the United States of America

Pivot Books are published by
Keats Publishing, Inc., 212 Elm Street,
New Canaan, Connecticut 06840

WHEAT AND SUGAR FREE
"What kind of title should that be?"
The family said to me
Then the local paper reads
"They're startling recipes!"
Another year, some more fuss
I hammered out *BLENDERBUSZ*
"We hope you're done,
Please don't write another one!"
The girls have got the woes
But Mother to the kitchen goes
The dishes clang, the pots are rattling
I don't say nothing, but the typewriters tattling
Oh, woe is me!
I guess I'm hooked
I just can't quit
Until my goose is cooked!

F.H.N.

Dedicated to my folks who were married in 1920, and especially my Dad, who, when I tried the recipes one more time before printing the books, washed for me dishes, dishes, dishes.

CONTENTS

THE NATURAL FOODS
BLENDER COOKBOOK

LETTING OUR HAIR DOWN

Recently there was an extension clubs' homemakers' fair in our town, where the speaker, a personality from the local radio station, gave a demonstration on the foods of the future. She gave a glowing account of the marvels to come in instant foods and time savers.

Now this is so ironic with the appliances that we modern women have in this day. What our grandmothers had to do the slow, tedious way with only arm power, we can do in seconds with the flick of a switch. Actually, even if you hold down a job every day, there is no excuse for using instant foods. Cooking from scratch or with natural ingredients is not time-consuming, if you have a little know-how and a few appliances.

Another ironic twist to this picture is the fact that when the husbands of these women or maybe even they themselves develop a heart or health problem, which is almost bound to happen on this type of diet, and it usually comes at a time in life when life is most enjoyable, they are told to get back to the natural diet and the doctor hands them booklets on preparing food right. So, the odds are that the biggest users of these convenience foods are forced to learn a different way of cooking, but then it may be too late. I'm sure if anyone, anywhere, takes a hard look around him at his friends and acquaintances, this is the picture that he sees. Now, most of us in our generation grew up in homes where mothers still gardened and cooked from scratch. So, if in later life they are put on a diet of no sweets, no fats, no processed foods, etc., they can adjust to it. But what about our children in their present generation where mothers are serving pop, kool aid, processed meats with the arti-

1

ficial flavors, and countless other instant and fast foods? All the flavor enhancers and things that are available are removing the real taste from food; and this present generation of children doesn't know how natural food should taste, nor will they be able to tolerate the change if they have to, for their health's sake. Just try changing now in your house: Cook a natural ground cereal in place of the dry packaged ones, and hear the howls from your kids. This you'll run into with every change that you make, until you can get them used to the change. When stopping at a drive-in for a hamburger once in a great while, I can't help but wonder about the future health of some of those pimply, dry-haired looking kids that support and work in these places and whose main diet is only this kind of food. They are in their youth, and anything goes. The mothers feel the same way. They are not thinking ahead to a world of widows, and even today a lot of mothers are burying their sons who have had heart attacks. In our area, all the small towns are populated with widows—lots of them. We women are at fault; we are killing our men. We rate each other's cooking on the basis of fancy desserts, fancy salads, that aren't salads at all and so on down the line. Even in our mother's day the home-baked bread on the table was the crowning glory, and a cook that put the vegetables fresh on the table without destroying them in some way was lazy or inferior.

Cooking that has no value is encouraged, admired, bragged about, and promoted. The easiest, simplest and most healthful way is frowned on and dare not even be discussed. Women that know better still feel that they have to serve certain things because everyone else does, or they don't want to appear different and invite gossip about themselves. Then, of course, there's always the argument that if things don't taste good and I can't enjoy eating, why live? Most women feel that if you start leaving out salt, sugar, chocolate, soda, chocolate chips, candies, white or cake flours, whipped cream substitutes—I could go on and on—there is nothing left and cooking is tasteless and impossible. What nonsense! That's when you first really learn to cook and things really start tasting good. At least I feel that way and that is what I am trying to prove. I hate the label "health foods." It should be thought of as better eating for that is what it really means.

As I think back, to when I was a little girl watching the cooking and preparing of food for daily use, or for weddings, anniversaries, threshing crews and events of that time, I remember some details: The women peeling apples for pies, standing nibbling on the peelings while they worked, the same with peeling potatoes. Even with the fresh vegetables that were served, they ate carrot pieces while they cut them up to soak in water. These are examples of what I'm trying to say: The women were eating the vitamins while the men were being served the "good stuff"—apple pies, or cooked-out applesauce, white fluffy mashed potatoes, and crisp vegetables with the vitamins all soaked out of them and left in the ice water. I don't believe that women are the stronger sex as they are saying now. The Bible says men are. If men are now the weaker sex, the women are making them that way and they start with habits instilled when boys and girls are little. Most women can't look at a bushel of apples without seeing them in pies, jelly, peeled and cooked some way. The same goes for any fresh fruit. I look at a box of fresh fruit and wonder how many days it will last, because our kids are so fond of fresh fruits that we only buy them to have them eaten fresh.

Can we reverse some of this trend and still be modern? Imagine giving a mother with a large family, back in the log cabin days, a blender, a mixer, range, automatic oven, running water, and refrigeration. Can't you picture her whirling away, grinding the whole grains, mixing the eggs and beating the batters. She would have the table and counter tops loaded with baked goods and foods in no time, foods made from real ingredients and having real values. Why can't we modern women do the same? Have we reached a point in cooking like one elderly lady said to me, "When one *doesn't* do anything any more, one *isn't* able to do anything any more."

ABOUT THE BOOK AND THE BLENDER

This book is a blender cookbook using what is generally considered health foods. I much rather would have it called cooking with natural ingredients, or from scratch. If you don't have some of these things in your kitchen, don't let that stop you from using these recipes. You can use the same amount of sugar as honey, or cocoa in place of carob powder.

As for the baking section in Part I, don't substitute there. You can adapt any of your own favorite recipes to the blender. Wheatless recipes are not easy to find, neither are 100% honey recipes. So leave them as they are when you want a special recipe using different flours. Whole-wheat and whole-rye flours can be used in any of the recipes in this book, however.

Any oil bought in the supermarket that you like can also be used as well as the cold pressed oils. Any mix seems to make up well in the blender. I have bought some to try because it's one of the questions usually asked when I am demonstrating blenders.

Again any recipe, even some of your oldest ones, can be made in the blender. One way is to blend all the liquid parts in the blender and the dry ingredients in a bowl and stir the two together.

There are some new ideas in blenders now, one is a

4

solid state blender. This type of blender will slow the speed down to where you can use it like a mixer. You can whip egg whites for example. Another new idea is a blender that has a heating element and will cook while it is blending. I have used four of the major brands in my kitchen and a solid state blender when demonstrating. The blenders that I own are from the cheapest to the medium priced range.

If you have a blender that turns apart on the jar base and fits a mason jar, you can double its use by ordering an extra knife assembly. That's the part that turns on the jar base. That way you can blend two parts of a recipe, one in the blender jar and one in a mason jar, without removing the base from the blender jar.

I can wreck a blender in a minute; I know just how to do it. One of the hardest things on a blender is sticky stuff like figs and dates. Don't be afraid to use them, but help along on the top. Shut the blender on and off and don't run it any longer than you have to with figs and dates. If they are hard, make them warm in the oven or with hot water. Any time a mixture gets thick, help along on the top with a spoon or rubber scraper and turn it off as soon as it's done, because it's hard on the blender if it runs a long time with such a heavy load.

If you are afraid something will be too hard on the blender like pressure cooked bones for example (Page 46), just cut through with a paring knife and throw the pieces in. If you can cut it with a knife the blender can, too.

There is a difference in repairing blenders should you find that you have to repair yours. A blender that is driven by a steel shaft will twist off below, in the blender base (where the motor is), and will have to be opened to replace it. It's not too difficult to do, though. Alton has always replaced ours if needed. A blender that is run by rubber-like fins on the bottom of the knives will twist off right there, if the blender load gets too heavy. Here the fin type gear twists off and a new one has to be turned on. The blender base does not have to be opened.

It's well worth a few extra dollars to have a blender that has a jar which turns apart on the base and allows you to use the same base on a mason jar. It not only makes for easier cleaning but it's more versatile. It's handy to be able to use a mason jar on the blender, and should something happen to your blender jar, you can use the blender until you get the jar replaced.

There are two types of blenders that fit mason jars. Some brands fit the regular mason jar and some fit the widemouth mason jar. If you are shopping for a blender, look around at both of these types before you decide. I hope I have not scared you and that you will not be afraid of using your blenders. That's what they are for. I doubt if anyone ever uses blenders harder than I do because I try anything and everything. Chances are that if you do have to repair yours, it won't be expensive. After all we have to change cars and other equipment too ever so often, and why not replace a blender if you've gotten a lot of use from one?

NATURAL FOODS

Let's talk a little about natural foods. When I use this term I don't mean an expensive protein supplement or glorified mixture available in special stores or supermarkets. I'm sure they are all right, I wouldn't know, because we don't use any of them. What I call natural foods are fresh vegetables, whole potatoes, not a dried or frozen variety, brown rice, fresh fruits, fresh meats, fresh eggs, fresh milk and cream, raw seeds, and anything along this line. Of course, this isn't 100% possible, because we can't spend 100% of our time in the kitchen. But we can bring it down to where we use as little as possible of canned foods, or cold meats and such. My main use of canned food is mostly to add a touch of flavor such as a can of pineapple to a fruit salad, or canned tomatoes for a salad dressing or meat sauce. We all are on our own and only in our own kitchens can we work out what to use less of or more of. Here are a few of the ways that I use food.

MEATS

I have our roasts cut as large as possible and all the meat put up in large packages on purpose, so that there will be some left over to eat cold. This I especially like for school lunches. A piece of cold roast or steak with a little vege-sal sprinkled on it is real good. Large roasts, a roaster full of stewing hens, goose, or ducks can be roasted during the night, if you work during the day, or in summer to keep down the heat during the day. There's nothing to it at all. Just lay your meat in the roaster, (I usually cover it), and set the automatic timer to go on about 4 or 5 in the morning. When you smell meat cooking it's about time to get up and check it to see if it's done. Now it's ready to slice and use cold, or use part of it cold and slice the rest and heat it in the gravy or meat juice. If you have a freezer and buy a whole or part of a beef or pork, etc., this is actually cheaper than cold meat. I do most of the meat baking at 325° or 300° when there is plenty of time. I have never timed it. I go by the size of the meat, if it is thawed out or not, and by smell. When it smells done, it usually is and when it smells burned it usually is; therefore when it smells good check on it to see if it is done. This is an art learned by experience and by how well done or rare you like your meat. If you cook by a timer and leave the meat in the oven, it continues cooking as long as the oven keeps its heat after it shuts off. A large roast cooked on a slow 300° heat is good roasted uncovered. It will get black or very dark outside and be juicy inside.

FOWL

Stewing hens, old roosters, a large goose, or one or more ducks, plain unstuffed, can be laid whole in a roaster and baked the same way as the roasts—either during the night or in a slow oven. You can serve some of them hot and put the rest away for cold eating. The breasts of duck and goose sliced thin, cold, are much like roast beef. A cheap stewing hen sliced cold is a real fooler for tasting like turkey. Fowl can also be cooked overnight in a large kettle and on low heat in an electric burner.

Add about half as much water as chicken. I don't bother to cut them up, I just put them in the pot whole. This cooked chicken makes a delicious broth and is good cold too. I'll go into this more later in Hen Blending. About this overnight business, I'm only stressing this to show a way of getting things done if you are busy during the day. It's ready and waiting when you come in after a day's work. It's also ready for the family if you aren't home. I'm going to add here something I like to do when having company noon dinners. For Thanksgiving or anything special we usually serve goose, duck or turkey. This is the last thing I do before going to bed the night before: Fill the bird with its stuffing and put it into the oven at 300°. But then, this only works if you go to bed late around 11 or 12 o'clock, which before a big day like that, with all the preparations, is usually late. Towards morning I wake up smelling it and check on it. Leave it in the oven after the oven is turned off and you can go to church with most of the meal finished. It will still be warm, but if you want it hot turn the oven on for a while after you come home, while you are getting the rest of the meal ready.

8

POTATOES

Are you in a big hurry and think cooking potatoes takes too long? It really can be done fast. First of all, they don't have to be scrubbed too clean if your time is short. Wash them quickly under running water and cook them. If cooked in a small amount of water in a stainless steel waterless pan, they don't take much longer than 15 or 20 minutes. Then just zip the peelings off and they can be served plain, mashed or creamed. Peeling hot potatoes is faster than peeling them before cooking. I keep a pair of rubber gloves just to handle hot potatoes easily. We cook all our potatoes in the skins. If you have them scrubbed clean, (this depends on the potatoes and the ground they were raised in, some are cleaner than others), you can cut them in small wedges and cook them in a little water and they are done real fast. In fact if time is that limited, start the water boiling while you are washing them. Then too, a large batch of potatoes can be washed and kept in storage until used.

ROOT VEGETABLES

There is a brush on the market that is sometimes hard to find. It has a handy curved handle for holding and the bristles are made of brass. But with it you are able to scrub carrots, potatoes, beets, or any root vegetables fast. This brush can be found in the housewares section of dime stores and supermarkets. A wad of nylon net works too, but not as well. A stainless steel kettle scrubber works fine, too. I feel I can clean and have fresh carrots, etc., ready in the same time it would take to open a jar, can or box of the vegetable. I have completely stopped canning and freezing root vegetables, but store them in stoneware crocks, covered in a cool place. We have an underground room off our basement where we store ours and these keep until late into spring. Don't put anything on them, no sand or dirt, just put them in a clean crock and cover. If you have a cool corner in your basement, they'll keep well too. I don't know if these crocks can still be bought in stores. I buy mine at auction sales, or maybe second-hand stores would have them. This year I also tried keeping them in plastic bags to see if that would work. Carrots kept particularly well by keeping the bag in a covered cardboard box. Beets, horseradish, winter radishes, turnips and parsnips are among the roots that store well.

JERUSALEM ARTICHOKES

Jerusalem artichokes have to be stored under dirt. These we dig and put in an old washtub, then cover them with the dirt that they grew in. They'll keep all winter this way. I dig some fresh if a nice day comes along and the ground thaws during the winter and early spring. They don't freeze all winter except for a few that grow too near the top of the soil. So they have to be dug ahead, but why go out when it's cold when you can have them in the basement in a tub? This dirt is handy to have too if you want to set out a house plant in the winter. But be sure and keep the cellar door shut if you have a house cat, because for some reason they are very fond of that dirt!

FRUIT

Fresh fruit can be bought all year. Why women knock themselves out canning expensive boughten fruit is a mystery to me. Why not buy what is available in season and eat plenty of it fresh? Why cook the value out of it and spend all that money on jars, caps, sugar and heat to can it? The only time I feel this makes sense is if you have your own fruit or if you can get some unsprayed fruit locally. There is always fresh fruit on the market, and that time and money can be used on other

10

things. It really doesn't cost any more to buy it fresh all year spreading the expense out, than to spend a lot at one time for canning.

I was told recently that peaches can be put in the freezer whole and frozen. I have put whole unpeeled peaches, pears, apples and halved or sliced muskmelon in the freezer. We think they are real good. The pears' skins turn a little dark, but after running hot water on them and peeling them, they are real good. All these frozen fruits peel very easy just by running hot water over them. They really taste good and fresh and if eaten while a little frozen, taste like a sherbet. They also are good in fruit salads and dishes of this type.

Apples also keep well in a cool place where you store root vegetables. Cherries freeze well raw and are easier to pit while slightly frozen.

OTHER FOODS

The emphasis in this book is on cooking fast, with natural ingredients or cooking from scratch. Almost anything made in the blender is an instant food.

FREEZING STRAIGHT FROM THE GARDEN

Here are some vegetables that can be frozen without blanching. All they need is to be cleaned, packed whole or cut up as desired.

Celery or celery tops
Cabbage, cut up for salads—and the outer leaves whole for cabbage roll-ups, etc.
Onions, small whole, cut-up, or tops
Cucumber either whole unpeeled, sliced or diced
Peppers—red or green, whole or cut
Parsley or any flavor leaves of any kind
Rhubarb should be cut up before packing

11

NATURE'S PERFECT PACKAGING

Peaches, pears, apples, cucumbers, peas, tomatoes, muskmelon, corn, anything that grows in a skin or peeling can be put into the freezer "as is" if the skins aren't broken. Some can be cut up to make them easier to handle such as muskmelon, which would be hard to cut up if frozen whole.

Tomatoes and Groundcherries—The small variety of tomatoes are a kids' pleaser frozen, as picked off the vine. If you can mix several varieties of small yellow and red ones and add some groundcherries still in the husks, it makes an attractive combination. They should be eaten frozen or slightly thawed. The large tomatoes can be frozen as you like, cut up or whole. The peeling slides right off under hot tap water. Keep a jar in your refrigerator thawing and ready for use when you need them.

Peas can be stuck in the freezer in the pods and shelled when needed, or used for adding to salads.

Corn—I don't think I'll bother freezing corn any other way any more. Just take off the roughest leaves and the tip of the tassel and freeze as fast as possible after picking. As long as no air gets to the kernels, it tastes like fresh corn. Give it several hours to defrost and roast on the open oven racks, still in the husks, at 400° until the husks are all charred dark brown. Of course, you can husk it and fix it any other way you like too, after defrosting. Be sure and leave on enough husks to freeze, only remove the few heavy outside husks.

FRUIT PUREES

On Page 75 there is a method given for freezing fruit purees or syrups made from red and dark fruits. These are also frozen raw.

Raw frozen foods are best used right away while still slightly frozen.

12

Part I

WHEAT AND SUGAR FREE

PRODUCTS USED

Here is a list of the products used in this book:

FLOURS

Rice
Oat
Soybean
Corn
Carob
Buckwheat
Rye
Wheat
Wheat germ (whole)

SEEDS AND NUTS

Brown rice
Raw wheat germ
Sunflower
Sesame
Poppy
Whole soybeans
Raw Pumpkin
Raw peanuts
Coconut

PRODUCTS

Cream-of-tartar-type
   baking powder
Vegetable oils
Pure flavorings
Rolled oats
Vegetables
Garden produce

FRUIT

Fresh
Dried
Your own
Wild

Unflavored gelatin
Dark whole-apple vinegar

Whole-wheat flour can be used in the recipes in this book. All recipes call for honey with the exception of two which call for raw sugar.

Oil means any liquid vegetable oil.

Gelatin is plain unflavored and is used extensively. It is too expensive to buy in the little packages. Order it by the pound.

The only leavening used in this book is cream-of-tar-tar-type baking powder, the baking powder made from grapes. No other kind is used or was tested in these recipes.

These products are available throughout the country in special stores. They also are available by mail through health catalogues. They are not expensive if you shop wisely. You can balance the budget by eliminating useless foods and replacing them with any of these.

ABOUT ADDING SUPPLEMENTS

Brewers' yeast, bone meal, and other supplements can be added to foods you are preparing. But a word of caution: they can break a dish, too. When you are cooking for children and add something that will make the dish distasteful to them, you gain nothing. They will have a distaste for that food that is hard to make them forget. It is far easier to get them to swallow a pill containing these things, which they don't taste on the way down. Here are some of the truths I have found out in adding supplements:

Brewers' yeast lends itself well to any product where you are using yeast such as buns, breads, etc. It actually improves the flavor if you don't overdo it. A little can be added anywhere you are using flours, but not so much that it will be detected.

Bone meal can be added to gravies, puddings, and of course anywhere you use a flour. Again not too much as it will get gritty. In a coarser product, such as corn meal, you can use more and get by with it. But if you can get the family to take six bone tablets every day, there's no problem adding it to the food.

Kelp can be mixed in with salt or salt seasoning. It blends in well in soup, gravy and things of that nature.

Wheat-germ oil can be added a drop or two every

16

time you use oil. This book has many recipes in which the oil stays raw and wheat-germ oil could be added.

ABOUT SEASONING

There is a little trick that I like to use concerning salt or seasoning. Instead of mixing it into the food, which one should never do, sprinkle it on top of the food just before serving. Or salt it at the table. This way the salt hits the tongue first and the food will actually taste saltier than it is. Most people have the habit of salting at the table whether you salted or not. Leaving salt till last will cut salt consumption down at your house. Everyone benefits from a lower salt consumption. Foods should never be cooked with salt added because it makes them weep and leaches out the vitamins. Keep the salt shaker away from the stove. If you are interested in what harm salt does to the body, read health magazines and publications. We get 'way too much salt. All commercially processed food is loaded with it, including ice cream and other sweet foods.

One of the best salt substitutes is vegetable seasoning. It is available in health stores and in catalogues is listed as salt seasoning. It is made of dried vegetables and gives flavor to everything. If we run out of that we use a savory or spice salt available locally

SCARED OF YOUR BLENDER?

Arm yourself with a wooden spoon and show it who's boss! Don't let it run you; you run it! Once it is in motion you can do most of your work with the cover off. Push and stomp down things like cabbage, seeds, etc., with your wooden spoon or scraper. Turning on and off, letting it come to a complete stop every time so it pulls down on the mixture, or stopping it and turning the ingredients so it catches new parts. Try anything and every way and you will succeed. Every brand of blender seems to act different after you get used to one. Just when you want to show someone how to do things, you'll find their blender acts differently and makes you look foolish.

Always start the blender with the cover on. Once it's in motion you can take the cover off to add ingredients or to help thick mixtures. Also put the cover on when you stop the blender as the contents tend to bubble up when it is turned off.

Always add flours while the blender is going. Otherwise flours will stick to the sides and make your job more difficult.

For success in grinding seeds it is best to start with at least 1 cup of seeds. If you don't have enough, they won't grind well.

Oils and eggs thicken in the blender, so if you want your mixture thin for better blending don't add these till the end. Oil seems to thicken in any protein in the blender.

For chopping turn the blender on and off quickly, watching closely to get the consistency you want.

Not all things blend (tomato seeds or raspberry seeds, for example). For special diets, strain foods when in doubt.

A blender whips gelatins almost double, but will not whip potatoes.

Watch hot mixtures as they come up and overflow easily. Give them plenty of room.

Add leavening at the last. That also starts to rise.

A blender will not whip eggs fluffy; it liquefies them.

Do not blend anything thickened with tapioca or tapioca flours. A blender thins them.

Use your blender for mixing the liquid part of any recipe. Put the dry ingredients in a bowl and pour the liquid over them.

Use your blender to make baby foods.

Use your blender for special diets. Even patients with touchy stomachs can enjoy the nutrients of most fruits when they are blended.

Use your blender for making nut and seed milks.

To clean the blender of sticky food, put some hot water in and turn it on.

Use your blender for liquefying homemade soap.

If there's any dry grinding to be done in a recipe, do it first so you won't have to wash and dry the blender between steps.

To make easier cooking gravies or custards, or anything that has a tendency to lump, first mix the thickening agent (flour, starch, or what you are using) with the liquid. Add to the hot mixture on the stove. It thickens fast this way. If anything is lumpy after the cooking, don't give it a thought. Just return it to the blender and unlump it. When hot mixtures are in the blender start on low then go to a higher speed or turn on and off very quickly to set in motion. Hot mixtures like to force the lid off and go over the top if you don't set them in motion slowly at first.

Another thing about "unlumping" hot mixtures: they will get thinner as they are blended, but will thicken again after they are poured into your bowl.

If blender is running and mixture is at a standstill, there are several things you can do. Stop blender completely, let bubble up, and restart. The blades will usually pull everything down this way.

Or, stop completely. Turn over the mixture with spoon or spatula so blender can grab new mixture.

Or, help mix with spoon or rubber spatula while running.

Or, turn on and off allowing blades to come to a complete stop each time.

To be able to work with the most efficiency with your blender, have a few helpers: wooden spoons, wire strainers, and rubber scrapers.

There are different finenesses in the screens of wire strainers. You really should have a few of the different sizes. To strain a whole blender full, have a large one that fits over a bowl or kettle. These come in finer and coarser screen. In working with fruits, such as cherries or grapes where you can blend seeds and all, have a large, finer one to hold back the broken pieces of seeds. If it is too small and too fine, you can't strain a puree. So get a larger strainer, but the finest screen available, in the medium large size. This is the one that you will use the most. Rubber scrapers are a must to get out all the dough. A long-handled, smaller one is good to get everything around the knife. Don't try too hard to get every bit out. I propped mine up once to drain every last bit out, and it slipped and broke on the sink. I'm not that prudent about getting that last bit out any more.

MR. NUSZ'S DON'TS

What wrecks a blender:
1. wife
2. lumpy, sticky stuff
3. shock load, which is a sudden load that won't fly apart, such as dried figs. After the blade is sticky as it is with figs or dates, it doesn't cut any more. Any food that won't shatter is hard on the blender. Strong hard steady loads will not hurt it. Only foods that won't shatter, the worst being dried figs and dates alone. As long as they're with a liquid, to keep the blade moving, or are cut into smaller pieces, the blender can cope. I never used to cut them up and ground a lot of dates and figs whole. But they were soft. I ran into trouble grinding whole dates and figs that were dried out.

20

MR. NUSZ'S RECIPE

2 cackleberries (eggs)
  flour
  honey
  oil
  and throw in a rubber scraper

He claims he's eaten many rubber scrapers already. I deny this although I have one that is scalloped on the tip and a wooden spoon with a few notches.

BASIC MIXES

MAGIC MILKS

Here I want to introduce you to magic-mix milks. These substitutes can be used in any recipe asking for milk in this book and I'm sure in any other. They are white as are other milks

No. 1

3 eggs, raw or cooked
½ cup oil

Turn blender on and keep adding water gradually. When blender is full, pour into a jar and add water to make about 4½ to 5 cups of milk.

No. 2

½ cup sunflower seeds
½ cup sesame seeds
3 cooked eggs

Add hot water gradually until thick and smooth. Keep

adding water to thin and when blender is full, pour into
jar and add enough water to make 4 or 5 cups of milk.
Sunflower alone is the mildest tasting. Use all sunflower
seeds for sunflower-seed milk.

No. 3

    1 cooked egg
    ¼ cup oil
    ⅓ cup water
    ⅓ cup brown rice, cooked

Blend until smooth. Add water to make 2 cups of milk.
This is the closest to cow's milk that I think it's possible
to come. This one is given in a smaller quantity to get
the rice blended well. It can be strained through a small
fine strainer to get it perfectly smooth. This one won't
separate as fast as the other two. They all can be used in
coffee to get the same taste as cream but will not look
the same.

The eggs can be cooked in part of the water and
added to the blender if you don't want to bother with
cooking them in the shell.

These milks will sour at about the same rate as cow's
milk.

MILLYUN DOLLAR MIX

    2 cups rice flour (unsifted)
    2 cups oat flour (unsifted)
    1 cup corn flour (unsifted)
    1 cup buckwheat flour (unsifted)
    1 cup soybean flour (unsifted)
    ½ cup wheat germ
    ¼ cup brewers' yeast powder
    ¼ cup bone meal powder

Mix well. Use for any recipe in this book calling for
flour. Use the same proportions as the recipe calls for.
For a pancake mix you could add a teaspoon of baking
powder for every cup of flour, although it's just as easy

to add it when you are mixing the dough. If you do want wheat, add a cup of whole-wheat flour to the above. I have never run across a pancake mix yet, health stores or what have you, that didn't have wheat flour in it. The reason for that must be an old idea that you have to have wheat to make things light. This just isn't true. You can make just as light, fluffy products with any of the above flours alone or in a mixture of two or more.

MAGIC MIX

This base of eggs, honey, and oil is used throughout the book. This to me is truly a magic mix because it lends itself to just everything. Any time you have some on hand you can make cookies, cake, pudding, frosting. It is complete, except for the baking powder, to pour over any flour and bake. You don't have to keep it on hand because it is so fast to make. This magic mix makes most of your baking instant.

    3 eggs
    1 cup honey
    1 cup oil
    1 teaspoon pure vanilla extract
    ¼ teaspoon pure almond flavoring

For baking add 1 teaspoon baking powder to every cup of flour. Pour over any flour, and bake. This is the recipe called for throughout this book when asking for Magic Mix. When amounts are changed instructions are given. If other flavorings are used, omit these given.

The customer complains, "This place is awful. The food is terrible. I demand to talk to the manager or the owner!"

The waiter says, "You'll have to wait awhile. He's out to lunch."

CAKES, COOKIES AND FROSTINGS
FROM BASIC MIXES

Before you start trying any of these, I want to say that you can use ANY flour in these recipes. Mix or use any of the flours that are listed in the beginning of *this* book. *Wheat germ* is used throughout the book.

Carob is used as cocoa and replaces part of the flour, about ½ cup to a cake.

Millyun Dollar Mix can be found on Page 22 and can be used in any recipe in place of flour.

Soybean flour is very successful used with Magic Mix. It makes a thicker dough than the other flours do, but bakes up light. It smells awful when you are mixing it up, but tastes real good in these recipes after it is baked.

Soybean flour when used with yeast is only good mixed in in small amounts. When soybean flour is used alone or if too much is used, yeast breads get soggy. But when it is used with baking powder it produces light and fluffy bread.

Refer once more to the Magic Mix at the start of this book. After you make a few things with it, you'll know it by heart and I'll wager that most of the time you won't need to look at a recipe any more.

Now I want to give any cake mix competition with cakes so fast that you won't be tempted to have mixes in the house "just in case I need one in a hurry." Have you ever wondered what keeps those mixes on the shelves for months without insects or spoilage? You can't do that with products at home that are free of any additives! Just try mixing up a good whole-grain flour with shortening and sugars and see how long it will keep for you.

Flours are **not sifted**—just a very full cupful taken as it comes. If flours are sifted the amount needed would be almost doubled.

MIX-ME-QUICK CAKES (ONE-STEP)

In blender:

    3 eggs
    ¾ cup honey
    1 teaspoon pure vanilla
    ¼ teaspoon pure almond

In bowl:

    1 cup of any flour (unsifted)
    ¾ cup oil
    1 tablespoon baking powder

Add in the order given. Pour blended mixture over dry ingredients in bowl; stir well. Bake all cakes at 325° to 350° till done. It's better to bake them slower and longer than at a high heat. If the bottom gets too dark, it spoils the flavor and they lose their moistness.

When using carob, use only vanilla flavoring.

When adding fruit, such as raisins, to the blender, you might not want to add flavorings to bring out the flavor of the fruit.

CAROB SOYBEAN

Use ½ cup soybean flour and ½ cup carob in above recipe; vanilla flavoring only.

If the flour lies on the top, just turn blender off and start it a few times. This usually pulls it down. Or be a helpalong and help stir on the top.

MAGIC MIX FOUR-EGG CAKES (TWO-STEP)

This makes a larger cake.

      4 eggs
      1 cup honey
      1 teaspoon pure vanilla
      ¼ teaspoon pure almond
      1 cup of oil

In bowl:

      1½ cups flour (unsifted)
      1 tablespoon baking powder

Pour blended mixture over dry ingredients and stir well. Bake.

FLUFFIER MAGIC-MIX CAKES

To make a spongier cake, separate the eggs and put only the yolks in the blender. Beat the egg whites very stiff in a mixing bowl. Add baking powder and beat again until high and creamy. Use either the one-step or the two-step recipes. Pour the flour over the egg whites and the blended mixture and fold in all at once. If you have any egg whites left over extra from another dish, add them here for a higher cake or jelly roll.

VARIATIONS USING FLOURS
(for both one- and two-step cakes)

Carob Rice

This is a cake everyone likes—good flavor. Use 1 cup unsifted rice flour and substitute ½ cup carob in place of ½ cup of flour.

Millyun Dollar

Good. This would make a good coffee cake. For topping see 3-Way Rice Cake. Use 2-step cake with 1½ cups Millyun Dollar Mix.

Rice Cake

Use all rice flour. Makes a coarser grained cake.

Slysoy Cake

Soybean flour is a sly one because it smells and tastes so awful in the raw state, but when you have this cake made up, you'll be pleasantly surprised at the fine texture and how the flavor changes. A word of caution: after using soybean flour wash everything you used because if you don't the next thing you make is apt to smell and taste like raw soybean, especially if it's something that you are not baking. I don't want to discourage you from buying soy products in health stores that are made for milk, etc. They are prepared for that and have a different taste.

Buckwheat Cake

Here's another that has a better flavor than you would think when done. Fine textured.

Oat Cake

This is good. Texture close to any yellow cake with white flour.

Wheat Germ

100 percent wheat germ and delicious!

Spice Cake

Use any combination of flours with spices used for any spice cake. Soybean flour is especially good with spices.

If I were to list all the combinations here that are possible, that alone could fill this book. Use what you want or what you have. I haven't had a failure with any combination yet.

Jelly Roll

Make the 2-step cake with oat flour. Separate the eggs and beat the egg whites stiff. Add baking powder and beat creamy. Fold in the blender mixture and the flour all at once. Spread out on a cookie pan that has the bottom lined with wax paper. Bake. Take out before too well done so the top is just a little sticky but the edges brown. The secret of a good jelly roll is not to bake it too dry. Loosen the sides and turn out on another wax-paper sheet. Spread with grape fluff or another jelly (see Jellies). Pick up the end of the wax paper and roll the cake into a roll. Scrape up the sticky crumbs that stayed on the paper and put them on the top of the jelly roll. Spread some more grape fluff over the top of all of this. Make jelly roll from other flours too.

THREE-WAY RICE CAKE

A cake to divide into three pans and make three different cakes! All three have the frosting baked right in!
In blender:

6 egg yolks
1 cup milk (your choice)
1 cup honey
1 teaspoon pure vanilla
2 cups unsifted rice flour
¾ cup oil

Blender mixture gets heavy. Help by stirring on the top with a spoon.
In bowl:

6 egg whites, beaten stiff
Sprinkle over when stiff 1 tablespoon baking powder. Beat high and creamy.

Pour blender mixture over egg whites and fold in.

Divide batter into three smaller pans, about 8″ x 8″. Make three variations following.

28

Ribbon Cake

Blend
    ½ cup honey
    ½ cup water
    ¾ cup carob
Pour or spoon crisscross over cake to make ribbons.
Bake 325° to 350°.

Carob Pudding Cake

Blend ½ cup honey, 1 cup water, and 1 teaspoon vanilla, and while blending add ½ cup carob. Pour over
cake and bake at 325°. Watch it and take it out right
when it's done, as the carob can scorch easily. Carob
pudding is at the bottom.

Cinnamon Coffee Cake

Chop ¾ cup sunflower seeds or nuts or mix mixture in
blender. Pour into bowl. Toss with ¼ cup honey and 2
teaspoons cinnamon. Crumble over cake batter. Use on
any cake that you want to turn into a coffee cake. Bake
at 325° to 350°.

Any of these variations can be baked into any cake in
this book.

GINGERBREAD

Make one batch Magic Mix, leaving out the flavorings. Pour into bowl. Stir in:
    ½ cup rice flour (unsifted)
    ½ cup oat flour (unsifted)
    2 teaspoons cinnamon
    ⅓ teaspoon allspice
    ⅛ teaspoon cloves
    ⅛ teaspoon nutmeg
    3 tablespoons molasses
    1 tablespoon baking powder
Stir well and bake.

Frost with a raisin frosting: Add 1 cup raisins and 1 teaspoon cinnamon to a cup of Magic Mix. Blend. Spread on hot cake.

GINGERBREAD COOKIES

Follow same recipe as above, only stir in enough flour to stiffen. Add raisins and nuts. Drop and bake.

SWEET NO-SWEETS
CAKES AND FROSTINGS

SPICE CAKE

Blend 6 large or 7 small eggs, 1 pound pitted dates (cut them up to make it easier on the blender). Turn on and off to chop, then blend. Add 2 cups oil and blend. In bowl:

    2 cups soybean flour (unsifted)
    1 tablespoon cinnamon
    1 teaspoon allspice
    1 teaspoon cloves
    1 tablespoon baking powder

Add:

    ½ cup cut-up dates
    ½ cup walnut pieces
    ½ cup raisins

Pour blender mixture over and stir well. Bake until done. 300°. Makes one large or two small ones.

CINNAMON FRUIT FROSTING

While cake is baking, blend:

    3 eggs
    ½ cup dates
    ½ cup raisins
    1 tablespoon cinnamon
    ½ cup oil

Blend by turning on and off to chop (on low if your

blender has low). Then blend. Spread on hot cake when cake is baked, or just before cake is done and finish baking with frosting on.

For a Christmas fruitcake use either the spice cake or butterscotch cake next. Add desired fruit, nuts, and seeds.

BUTTERSCOTCH CAKE

3 eggs
1 cup dates
1 teaspoon vanilla

Turn on and off, then blend until smooth. Add 1 cup oil. Pour into bowl and add 1 cup rice flour and 2 teaspoons baking powder. Bake.

QUICK MIX BANANA CAKE

3 eggs
1 cup honey
3 bananas, cut up
  vanilla or lemon flavoring (just a few drops of lemon)
½ cup oil

Blend smooth.

½ cup walnuts

Turn on and off only enough to chop nuts a little.
In bowl:

1 cup rice flour (unsifted)
1 cup soybean flour (unsifted)
1 tablespoon baking powder

Pour blender mixture over flours and mix well. Bake at 325°.

RICH CAROB CAKE DESSERT

3 eggs
1 cup honey
1 teaspoon vanilla
½ cup rice flour and ½ cup carob flour added while blender is running (unsifted)
1 cup oil
1 tablespoon baking powder

Add in order given while blender is running. Help with spoon at end. Bake in 8″ x 8″ pan at 325°.

Fill depressions on top with cut-up marshmallows (see Confections). Prepare instant cooked egg carob pudding (see cooked egg puddings), and pour over top. Let set a couple of hours to blend flavors.

SPONGE CAKES
(2 bowls)

6 egg yolks
1 cup honey
vanilla and almond flavorings

While blending add:
1 cup oil

In bowl:
1 cup rice flour (or other)

Add blender mixture and mix well.

Beat the 6 egg whites very stiff, add the 1 tablespoon baking powder and beat high and creamy with mixer. Pour over flour and blender mixture and fold in by hand.

CAROB SPONGE

Same as above except not quite a cupful of honey because of carob sweetness. Use ½ cup carob and ½ cup rice flour.

COOKIES

BASIC COOKIE RECIPE

    1 batch of Magic Mix
    4 cups flour (unsifted)
    1 tablespoon baking powder
Mix well. For rolled cookies, add flour until stiff. Chill.

FOR BABY

    To bake a hard cookie for baby, make dough very stiff with flour (soybean for protein). Add a tablespoon of bone meal powder to the flour.

ANISE COOKIES

A licorice flavored treat for the kids!
    1 batch Magic Mix with 1 teaspoon anise flavoring blended in
In bowl:
    1 cup of each of the following, unsifted:
       rice flour
       oat flour
       soybean flour
       wheat germ
    1 tablespoon baking powder
    3 tablespoons anise seeds
Pour the Magic Mix over the flour. Mix well. Drop by spoonfuls on buttered cookie sheet. Sprinkle top with anise seeds. Bake at 350°.

DATE FROSTING

    2 eggs
    1 cup dates
Chop and blend smooth. Add:
    1 teaspoon vanilla
    ½ cup oil
Spread on cake while hot. Makes 18 cupcakes.

CAROB BROWNIES

    3 eggs
    1 cup dates
    4 tablespoons carob
Chop, then blend smooth. Add 1 cup oil. Pour into bowl and add:
    2 teaspoons baking powder
    1 cup rice flour (unsifted)
    1 cup broken nut meats
Bake in 9" x 9" pyrex pan.

CAROB DATE FROSTING

    1 egg
    ½ cup dates
    1 tablespoon carob
      vanilla
    ½ cup oil
Chop and then blend smooth. Spread on hot cake.
    These frostings can be used on any cake.

SELF-FROSTING BARS OR COOKIES

Self-frosting means to make one batch of Magic Mix, using two-thirds of it for the dough and one-third for the frosting. Pour Magic Mix into a bowl and leave, or pour back into the blender one cup of the Magic Mix. In the bowl stir up the bars or cookies; in the blender, mix the frosting. For bars: add 2 cups of flour and 2 teaspoons baking powder to bowl mix. For cookies add 3 cups of flour and 2 teaspoons baking powder to bowl mix.

FESTIVE OATMEAL BARS

Make one batch Magic Mix using only vanilla flavoring. Pour all but one cupful into a bowl. Leave one cupful in blender.
In bowl:
Add 3 cups rolled oatmeal and 1 teaspoon baking powder to the Magic Mix. Spread in well buttered baking pan, 8" x 8".

FESTIVE FROSTING

Now to the Magic Mix left in the blender add 4 tablespoons carob. This makes the frosting. Spread on top of oatmeal in the pan. Bake at 350°. When done cut into bars. This one cup of Magic Mix and 4 tablespoons carob can be frosting on any cake.
Variations: Add nuts, seeds, coconut, in place of one cup of oatmeal. To make festive all-carob bars, add 3 tablespoons carob to oatmeal batter.

FIVE VARIATIONS FOR SELF-FROSTING

1. Spread on hot cake when done.
2. Dribble over the top and let bake into the batter.
3. Let bake until almost done. Spread frosting on top and finish baking.
4. When cookies are done, but still hot, make thumb print deep in the middle to make hole and fill.
5. Fill teaspoon with frosting or filling and push down hard on center of unbaked cookie to make hole and push filling in. Bake.
Bake as bars or cookies. Cut into bars when done.

FIG SELF-FILLED BARS OR COOKIES

Make one batch of Magic Mix. Pour all but one cupful into bowl. Leave the rest in the blender. Add 2 cupfuls of flour and 2 teaspoons of baking powder to bowl for bars, or add 3 cupfuls and 2 teaspoons baking powder for drop cookies. Mix well. Add figs cut into fourths slowly to Magic Mix in blender. Chop and blend. Add figs until thick. (Use soft ones to make it easier for your blender.) Add ½ cup of cut-up figs to this mixture when done. Also add ½ cup to the dough if desired. Make variations listed above.

POPPY SEEDS SELF-FROSTED

Same procedure as above using your choice flour. Add ½ cup of whole poppy seeds to the dough, ½ cup poppy seeds to the frosting. Let them blend a long time to grind them up. Make whatever variation you like above.

SESAME SEEDS SELF-FROSTED

Same as poppy seed. To keep seeds raw, put on cookies or bars when they are baked but still hot. Add sesame seeds to frosting until thick. Blend.

Hint: Toast one cup of sesame seeds in hot frying pan. (See how under Nuts and Seeds). Add to your jar of raw seeds for more flavor.

SOYBEAN-SESAME BARS

Make bars of 100% soybean flour. Blend self-frosting with sesame seeds of which one cup is toasted.

SPECIAL SOYBEAN SPICE

Make one batch Magic Mix and pour into bowl leaving the one cup in the blender. Leave out all flavorings.

For cookies or bars, use 2 cups flour to mix with Magic Mix in bowl. Soybean thickens faster than other flours, so use only 2 cups for cookies, too. Add 2 teaspoons cinnamon and ⅛ teaspoon each nutmeg, allspice, and cloves Mix well.

Filling: Add one cup raisins to Magic Mix left in blender. Blend until thick. Add 1 teaspoon cinnamon. Make round holes in cookies and fill. Bake at 350°. I'm sure you'll like these.

OTHER FILLINGS OR FROSTINGS

All of these so far can be used as a frosting on any cake or cookie. Use one cup of Magic Mix and start adding and mixing to your satisfaction.

Apricot

Add dried apricot pieces to the mix, both filling and dough.

Raisin

Add one cup of raisins to the batch of Magic Mix. Also add some to dough if desired.

Raisin Cinnamon

Same as above only add 1 teaspoon cinnamon each to the filling and the dough.

Prune

Add prunes to both dough and filling or just to the filling.

Nut

Add ground nuts toasted and raw to Magic Mix to make it thick. (See how to toast under Nuts and Seeds.)

Raw Jellies

Cranberry, strawberry, cherry, or grape. Follow directions for making under Jellies. Do not add to Magic Mix.

~CAROB COOKIES

    1   batch Magic Mix with vanilla flavoring
    ¾   cup carob
    1   cup rice flour (unsifted)
    1   cup oat flour (unsifted)
    1   cup wheat germ
    1   tablespoon baking powder

Pour Magic Mix over, mix well and bake. Frost with carob frosting or leave plain.

VARIATIONS FOR ABOVE

Mix up 2 cups combined flours, add nuts, bake, cut into brownies.
    Top with nut meats.
    Add chopped dates
        sunflower seeds
        sesame seeds
        coconut.
Drop into ground nuts to coat; bake.

FILLED COOKIES

Make basic cookie recipe—1 batch Magic Mix to 4 cups flour mixed with 1 tablespoon baking powder.
    Drop on buttered cookie sheet by tablespoons. Drop a teaspoon of filling on that. Then drop a teaspoon of dough on the filling. Or push filling down into the cookie with the spoon and leave it open-faced. Top with nut meat.

FILLED FIG BARS

Add enough flour to Magic Mix to make it stiff. Chill. Roll out on floured board or between 2 sheets of wax paper—the rolling pin won't stick. Or roll out on arrowroot flour. This works well because it's such a slippery flour. For fig or date bars roll out and spread filling down the middle, bring the two sides together, and close it up. This is easy to do if you rolled it on wax paper. Flop the whole thing over on your cookie sheet so the closed edges are on the bottom. Bake at 325° so the dough stays soft and browns only lightly. When done, cut the roll jelly-roll fashion for bars.

For me this is altogether too much work. Cookies taste just as good dropped and you have half the work.

OPEN-FACED COOKIES

Roll out dough on wax paper. Slide the whole thing on a cookie sheet, wax paper and all. Spread filling evenly over the top, and bake slowly. Cut in different shapes.

PLAIN FILLINGS FOR FILLED COOKIES

1 egg
⅓ cup oil
⅓ cup hot water
figs or raisins

Turn blender on and off to chop, then blend. Add figs or raisins until thick. Cut up figs to make mixing easier on the blender. Use only soft ones because hard ones can wreak havoc on it. (See other fillings under Self-Frosted Bars.)

SWEET NO-SWEETS RAISIN COOKIES
(Sweetened only with raisins)

2 eggs
2 cups raisins
2 tablespoons molasses

Blend until smooth and thick as these blended raisins are what sweeten the cookies. Pour into bowl; add:

1 cup oil
1 cup whole raisins
¼ teaspoon each cloves and nutmeg
3 teaspoons cinnamon
1 tablespoon baking powder
2 cups oat flour (unsifted)
1 tablespoon bone meal (optional)
    nuts (optional)

Mix well. Drop by spoonfuls on oiled cookie sheet. Top each with walnut half. The flavor improves after they are allowed to mellow by storing a day or two. These freeze well.

About adding bone meal: cookies are a good place to get by with it. Since cookie dough is usually a heavy dough, and so are the cookies, the bone meal is hard to detect. Now having read in the health books of oats or oatmeal being hard on the calcium in your system, why not add it when you are using oat flour? It does not cause an emergency with your calcium, I'm sure, but since we do know about it, we can discourage the problem. The bone meal powder is as fine as a flour in case you're not familiar with it.

PEANUT COOKIES OR BARS

First grind raw peanuts one cup at a time in blender. Toast one cup in hot frying pan. (See how to toast under Nuts and Seeds.)

1 cup Magic Mix
1 teaspoon baking powder
2 cups ground peanuts

Drop on buttered sheet or pour into 8″ x 8″ pan. Frost if desired with peanut Magic Mix frosting. Bake at 325°. Makes one dozen. For more all-nut and seed cookies, look under Nuts and Seeds.

PEANUT MAGIC MIX FROSTING

Mix ground (part toasted) peanuts with one cup Magic Mix until thick. A tablespoon of peanut butter can be added, too.

BONE MEAL COOKIES FOR BABIES
(Soft)

    2 eggs
    1 cup pitted dates, blend smooth
    ½ cup oil
Pour in bowl; add:
    3 tablespoons carob
    1 cup bone meal powder
Bake at 325° until done or set. Eating one per day is enough.

MATRIMONY BARS

Make one batch Magic Mix. While in blender add 1 cup oat flour and 1 tablespoon baking powder.
In bowl:
    3 cups regular or quick rolled oatmeal
Pour blender mixture over and mix well. Spread half of it in the bottom of the pan.
In blender:
    2 cups dates (cut them up to make blending easier)
    1 cup hot water
Turn blender on and off to chop, then blend. Spread over bottom layer of oatmeal mixture in pan. Spread the rest of the oatmeal mixture over that. Bake. Cut into bars.

VARIATIONS FOR ABOVE

Add nut meats.
Sprinkle top with cinnamon.
Use other fruit for filling.

A salesman comes into a restaurant early in the morning and the waiter says in a gruff voice, "What'll you have?"

The salesman says, "Give me a couple of eggs and a few kind words."

Later the waiter comes and says, "Here's your eggs."

The salesman says, "Where's my kind words?"

The waiter leans over and says, "Don't eat those eggs!"

FROSTINGS

MAGIC MIX FROSTINGS

Use one cup Magic Mix or:
  1 egg
  ⅓ cup honey
  ⅓ cup oil
  pure flavorings

Pour into bowl. Add ground nuts, sunflower seeds, fruits, wheat germ, poppy seed, ground nuts, toasted ground nuts, sesame seeds, toasted sesame seeds, pumpkin seeds, carob, sunflower seed meal, sesame seed meal, etc. Use one alone or vary with mixtures. For better flavor when using raw seeds, toast part of them and add the rest raw. Toast in hot frying pan stirring steadily until browned. Also vary with flavorings: anise, lemon, almond, vanilla, spices. Also vary with fruits. Add to blender mixture and blend until thick. Add some cut-up and chopped after blending. Raisins are especially good. Put on cooled, hot, unbaked or partly baked cake.

SMOOTH CREAM FROSTINGS

1 cup Magic Mix or:
⅓ cup honey
⅓ cup oil
1 egg
   vanilla
4 tablespoons carob

Add carob while blender is running. Start and stop to pull under if it lies on the top.

FLUFFY CAROB FROSTING

Combine 1 cup honey, ¼ cup water, ⅔ cup carob. Bring to a boil, turn down heat and let simmer. Meanwhile beat six egg whites until very stiff. Pour the boiling mixture over the egg whites beating hard. Add vanilla and beat in. Makes a large amount of frosting.

BROILED FROSTING OR CANDY COOKIES

Use the 6 egg yolks from the Fluffy Carob Frosting. Add 1 cup honey, ½ cup oil, and vanilla and almond flavorings. Blend all these. Pour into a bowl and add:

   ½ cup wheat germ
   1 cup coconut
   1½ cups ground nuts and toasted ground peanuts
   1 cup whole mixed nuts

Spread on cooled cake and broil. Or spread on hot cake and broil. If you have any frosting left over, it is good chilled and then formed into little balls for candy. Or, drop them by teaspoonfuls on a buttered cookie sheet and bake at 350° until brown. Very good little cookies.

BROILED PLAIN FROSTING

Mix 1 cup honey, ½ cup oil and 1 teaspoon vanilla in blender. Mix with about 2 cups mixed nuts, coconut, etc. Spread on cake and broil. Makes a cake nice and moist as it soaks in.

BROILED EGG FROSTING

Same as above only add 1 egg to blender mixture.

Variations: cinnamon, carob, any whole or ground nuts, wheat germ, etc.

RICE FROSTING

4 eggs
¾ cup oil
¾ cup honey

Blend and add:

4 tablespoons carob
1 cup cooked brown rice

Blend until smooth and thick. Spread on and between cake layers.

APPLES

This is not a blender recipe but a delightful tray to pass around or to precede a meal. Quarter apples, do not peel. Remove core, stick a toothpick into each quarter. Dip into thawed frozen orange juice and coat. Arrange on clear glass dish or tray. Very pretty! Guests eat them on the toothpick.

PINEAPPLE RAW APPLESAUCE

In blender:
    1 cup pineapple juice (drained) or crushed pineapple

Fill blender with unpeeled apple pieces. Turn on and off to chop, then blend as fine as wanted. Use fresh or frozen apples.

ORANGE RAW APPLESAUCE

In blender:
    1 can frozen orange juice (thawed)

Fill blender with unpeeled apple pieces. Turn blender on and off to chop, then blend as fine as wanted. When using frozen apples you have an apple ice.

COOKED APPLESAUCE

For an easy cooked applesauce, cook the unpeeled, cored, apples. Throw into blender with cooking liquid and blend.

Variations: cinnamon on all of these.

Hint: To keep raw applesauce in the refrigerator or freezer, cover the top with crushed pineapple or orange juice. Try making only enough for the meal.

BEETS

COOKED BEETS

Wash and clean beets. Do not peel; cut away only what you have to. Cut into strips with fancy cutter or leave plain. Cook with:

   ½ cup honey
   ½ cup vinegar

Cook until barely done. Do not cook too soft. Turn heat to high, then to low. Keep tightly covered. Never let steam escape when cooking vegetables.

Variations: Make beet relish and use juice from that for cooking these. Thicken juice with cornstarch or arrowroot flour.

For a cooked relish, make another blender of relish when you are serving a raw one, and cook the last one with the juice. Thicken if desired.

See also Raw Beet Relish under Relishes.

BONES

BONES MAKE GOOD BROTH STOCK

Reprinted from *Prevention*, May, 1965

Do you want to be thrifty and still serve nourishing food? Then try canning bones! When we have our beef wrapped and cut, I ask the butcher to cut the bones small enough to go into a widemouth Mason jar.

Simply pack the jar full of bones and fill with water. They don't have to be packed in tight. Close the jars and process them in a pressure cooker at 10 to 12 pounds of pressure. I try to keep the pressure between 10 and 15 pounds. Process about 2 or 3 hours. The longer and the higher the heat at which they are cooked the softer they become. Also more gelatin cooks out into the liquid. The liquid in the jars will become stiff with gelatin. The fat rises to the top and is lifted off when you open the jar.

Set the jars on your shelves for instant meals. For quick soup you can add tomatoes, vegetables, onions, brown rice, or whatever you like or have on hand. I sometimes add browned hamburger for extra flavor.

For bone meal patties: Fill the blender half full with the contents from the jar (bones and all). Add eggs until it blends well. Let it blend until the bones are blended in. Pour into a bowl, add onion, seasoning, and regular rolled oats. Add the oatmeal until it's thick enough to spread and the patties will hold the shape. Brown the patties on both sides in cooking oil.

If there is a bone that refuses to blend, simply pick out those pieces and throw away. There are some bones that don't get soft, but those like the ribs, etc., can be easily eaten. If they have some meat on them and have not been trimmed too close, they are even better. This method also supplies the bone marrow.

One last word—It has to be a pressure cooker as the heat does not get high enough by any other cooking method. This could also be done in a small pressure cooker for one meal at a time.

I got started on this because I needed to save freezer space and hated to see those bones thrown away because of the value in them.

Mrs. Frieda Nusz

Hint: Cut up bones with a knife by hand before putting in blender. Discard really hard ones.

"BLIVER"

Reprinted from *Prevention,* February, 1966

Mrs. Frieda Nusz will never know all that happened because she shared her blender recipes with *Prevention* readers, but when the meat ran low in our home freezer recently, I recalled her article, "Bones Make Good Stock" in the May issue of your magazine, and decided not to wait for butchering time to blend some bones.

I bought a pound and a half of neck bones, pressure-cooked with plenty of water for about two hours; put about two cups of the cooking liquid in the blender, and added the bones with their meat. These bones blended uniformly, resulting in a thin gravy which went well with our boiled-in-their-jackets potatoes.

The leftover bone gravy solidified in the refrigerator. When sliced it reminded me of liver loaf. This set me thinking. We love liver loaf, but suspect it has additives not healthful. So—maybe I could make our own.

I bought two pounds of neck bones and one of liver. The neck bones were cooked as before, blended with two cups of the broth, and poured into a bowl. Meanwhile I had stewed the liver in a covered saucepan until done. I dropped in a pinch of rosemary leaves to cook with it. Into the blender went about two cups of cooking liquid and the liver. When well blended, this was stirred into the bone mixture. It became a very stiff loaf after a few hours in the refrigerator. This is Bliver at our table.

No doubt this product can be improved upon. I plan to use different proportions of bones, liver, and water, also various mixtures of herb seasonings, until the loaf suits us perfectly.

But I just couldn't wait to share my find with *Prevention's* creative cooks!

Mrs. Clyde Long
Cashion, Oklahoma

CABBAGE

For salads look under Salad and Salad Dressings.

CABBAGE JUICE
(for ulcers)

Fill blender with coarsely cut-up cabbage. Needs at least three handfuls to work properly. Start blender—push down with rubber scraper to keep cabbage going into blade. After it gets like cole slaw, turn blender on and off to work it into a mush. When it starts to juice let it run until it's good and mushy. This might be soft enough so that your stomach will tolerate it this way. For juice, pour into screen wire strainer. Press juice out with rubber scraper. This is a real green juice. I must say it's not very tasty. We don't have ulcers so don't have to drink it, but I found out a little honey makes it taste pretty good.

CAROB

Carob is what we know as St. John's bread. The sweet pods are available at Christmas time. It is believed that these pods are what St. John lived on in the wilderness. In that region of the world the tree they grew on is known as a locust, hence the locusts and wild honey of the Bible. The tree's name is caruba. In the November, 1960, issue of *Organic Gardening,* Gertrude

Springer in her *Home on the Range* column says, "Many questions come to me about this natural sweet which I will now try to answer. The powder tastes like cocoa. Rather than being hard on the kidneys and liver like cocoa, it is rich in calcium, phosphorus, potassium, magnesium and the wonderful B vitamins which keep the digestive tract healthy. In fact, carob powder is used by physicians to overcome digestive ailments, especially in babies. It has its own B vitamins and doesn't have to rob the body of them during digestion, as do the commercial sugars.

"Until you have learned to like the slightly different taste of carob, use a little less than you'd use of cocoa."

CONFECTIONS

CANDIES FROM SEEDS

First step: make coatings for seed candies.

Chop walnuts, peanuts and coconut in the blender separately. Pour these into deep cereal bowls for rolling and coating the candies.

To chop nuts: Turn the blender on and off quickly until they are the way you want them.

To chop coconut: You will have to keep pushing it down on the sides of the blender with a rubber spatula until it is as fine as you want it.

Separate the nuts into two bowls. Leave one plain; add cinnamon to the other. Separate the coconut into two bowls; leave one plain and add carob powder to the other.

Have plain carob in one bowl.

A heaping tablespoon of honey in these recipes means swirling the spoon until you can lift it to the bowl without dripping. This actually is more than a level tablespoon.

For making ahead, freeze all of these separately on a cookie sheet. Then throw them into freezer containers to store in the freezer.

SUNFLOWER SEED CANDY

Blend 2 cups sunflower seeds to a fine meal. Start with cover on and then remove cover and push seeds down with spatula. Always do this carefully, keeping far away from the knife. Add 1 tablespoon each honey, butter and vanilla, to one cup of the ground seeds; add 1 heaping tablespoon peanut butter and vanilla to the other cup. Form into balls and roll in coating mixtures.

SESAME SEED CANDY

2 cups sesame seeds
½ cup oil

Start blender with cover on and run it a while. Take the cover off and help push seeds down and under. Add 2 tablespoons honey and a dash of vanilla. Divide into three bowls. Add 1 tablespoon peanut butter to one and 1 tablespoon carob to another; leave one plain. Shape into balls. Do not coat these. They resemble fudge.

SESAME TAFFY

1 cup sesame seeds
⅛ cup oil
2 tablespoons honey
vanilla and a bit of almond flavoring

Start blender and help seeds turning down and under with rubber scraper. Let it run a long time until mixture gets hot and looks glossy. Turn out into bowl. With rubber scraper knead up on side of bowl, squeezing out the oil. Finish kneading with your hands squeezing out the oil. Roll this dough into a log and slice.

51

PUMPKIN SEED CANDY

Dry blend:
  2 cups pumpkin seeds
Add:
  2 tablespoons honey
  ½ cup of oil from sesame taffy (optional)
     dash pure vanilla extract
Drop by teaspoons into coating mixtures. Chill.

LICORICE CUBES

  6 tablespoons gelatin
  2½ cups hot water
  2 tablespoons licorice root pieces or tea pieces
Blend to release flavor. Add:
  1 teaspoon anise flavoring
Add one cup of hot water to start and keep adding the
rest gradually. The blender gets pretty full and will
foam up. Then add the anise flavoring (it takes the
foam back down). Strain the blender contents through a
cloth and discard it. Let set for a while to give any foam
a chance to rise to the top. Skim off the foam and pour
into a square freezer container. Refrigerate until good
and stiff. Run hot water over the back of the container
till the block of licorice falls out. Cut into small cubes.
For keeping, spread out on a cookie sheet and freeze.
Later throw into a freezer container. They turn white
when frozen. Defrost for eating. The natural color of
these is yellow. My tasting panel of four say they taste
as good as the red, yellow, black or what have you in
the stores. Keep at room temperature.

PEPPERMINT CUBES

Follow same recipe and procedure above, except
blend in a handful of fresh peppermint leaves in place
of the licorice. Add a teaspoon of pure peppermint flavoring at the end.

These turn black or rather dark colored after they are done. In other words, these look like licorice and the licorice looks like peppermint. At least that's the colors that we have become used to, even if they are not the true natural color of the food.

CHRISTMAS CANDY LOGS

We have made these for years. Everyone asks for the recipe and when you tell them it's only dates they find it hard to believe. In these, grinding the dates through a food or meat chopper seems to change the flavor and the appearance of the dates.

In blender:

Chop 2 cups of coconut very, very fine. Keep pushing it down the sides to get it finer. Put in bowl.

In chopper:

Grind as many pitted dates as you want. If they are the dry pressed ones grind them alone. If they are the moist ones throw in some coconut once in a while. Run some coconut through when you are done to clean the chopper of dates. Knead this into a dough with your hands. Roll into long strips on cutting board and cut into logs. Or shape into anything you dream up. Coat by rolling in coconut. These can be formed into knots, twists, balls, or what have you.

The kids have a ball with these. They enjoy the grinding, shaping, and everything. Most stores carry unsweetened coconut at Christmas time. It is also available in health stores and catalogues all year.

HEALTH MARSHMELLOS

1 cup water

Pour about ¾ cup of this water into a little saucepan and let come to a boil. Meanwhile mix 2 tablespoons cornstarch in the cup with the remaining cold water. Stir this into the boiling water. It thickens at once. Add:

½ cup honey
1 tablespoon pure vanilla
¼ teaspoon almond flavoring

to the hot mixture. Set it in the freezer and let it get good and cold or part frozen. When it's cold, put into blender:

1 cup warm to hot water
3 tablespoons gelatin

Blend until high and fluffy and gelatin is melted. Add cold cooked mixture by spoonfuls and let it whip up. If it gets thick in the blender add a little cold water to keep it going. Now you can add a teaspoon of baking powder and the mixture will fluff up more. This is optional. The candy is good either way—lighter for eating with the baking powder, but stiffer without for adding to salads, puddings, etc. Pour the mixture in a pyrex cake pan and set it to get good and cold. The candy is easier to work with when it is good and stiff. When cold cut into cubes or squares. Have a deep dish with arrowroot flour beside you. Drop mellos into the flour and coat them well. Spread them out on a cookie sheet to dry. From this point on keep them at room temperature. After they dry and the coating absorbs some of the sweetness, they will taste quite similar to the commercial variety. Do not pack in plastic bags as they don't have preservatives added to them and will mold. Keep in an open dish, and when they are good and dry, they will roast like all marshmallows. They are good roasted under the broiler. Use them to melt over cookies or broil on a cake.

MARSHMELLO TOPPING

Follow directions for making marshmellos. In bowl whip three egg whites very stiff. To the marshmello in the blender add and blend in ½ cup oil. Pour over the stiff egg whites. Fold in by hand. Keep at room temperature or it will get too stiff. Stir to soften. Use leftover topping as marshmellos. It gradually thickens and sets.

QUICK TOPPING

Blend 2 egg whites in blender; add marshmellos to running blender until container is half full. Add ½ cup oil. Blend and serve.

FUDGEMELLOS

Everything stays uncooked in this concoction.
 1 cup hot water
 2 tablespoons plain gelatin
Blend up until white and fluffed; add
 2 egg yolks
 ½ cup honey
 5 tablespoons carob
 ⅓ cup oil
 ½ cup chopped nuts
Beat the egg whites stiff in a bowl and pour blender mixture over, folding in well. Pour into pan, chill until very stiff. Cut into squares. Can be rolled in chopped nuts and kept at room temperature for short intervals.

CORN

Putting up corn is one of the major events of the summer. I freeze and can it. This past summer on a day when I was swamped with it, I remembered reading about freezing it in the husks. So I laid one shelf full of corn just as it came from the field. Well it is the middle of February and we just ate some and it tasted the closest to fresh corn you can eat in winter time. This could be a real time saver for women who are busy.

Lose as little time as possible between the garden and the freezer, as corn loses its sweetness rapidly. Some people have the water boiling when they go to get it!

CREAM-STYLE CORN

An easy shortcut to making cream-style corn with your blender! Put about half of your canned, fresh or frozen whole kernel corn in the blender. Add some of the cooking liquid and blend it. Add to the whole kernel and cook in the usual way. I like to add about ½ cup milk, 1 teaspoon honey, ½ teaspoon seasoning and a pat of butter to a pint of corn.

MEXICALI CORN

Put about 1 cup or more of the cooking liquid from the corn in the blender. Throw in pieces of pimento and green peppers and turn on and off to chop. Add to the corn and prepare like cream-style corn.

CORN MEAL

We are lucky enough to live near "the Sioux Miller" of Sioux City, Ia. The corn meal he grinds is from open pollinated corn. It is fine and golden.

TORTILLAS

The dictionary says a tortilla is a flat corn cake baked on a hot iron. So here is a flat corn cake baked on your griddle or in a frying pan in a little butter. Serve these with Tavern Meat or a slice of Delux Meat Loaf, hot or cold. Put meat on half of the tortilla and fold the other half over it like a sandwich. (For meat recipes look under Tomatoes.)

    3 eggs
    1 cup corn meal
Blend until thick and add:
    1 cup hot water

Pour on hot griddle or in hot butter. Brown on both sides. Stir batter before pouring each time. These can also be eaten as pancakes.

When we were in Tucson, Arizona, friends of ours served these with browned hamburger sprinkled over, then a dry tossed salad, cut fine, sprinkled over that, and on top of all that a dressing was poured over. Any of your favorite tomato dressings would be good. (They used the commercial tortillas browned in oil.)

JOHNNY CORN CAKE
MIX-ME-QUICK CORN CAKE

    3 eggs
    1 cup milk (your choice)
    1½ cups corn meal
Turn blender on and add:
    ½ cup oil
    1 tablespoon baking powder
Turn on and off until it's all pulled down. Let it come to a complete stop until it bubbles up, then turn on. In this way it pulls down from the top. Pour into 8″ x 8″ pan and bake.

CORN CAKE
(2-Step)

    3 eggs
Separate the whites into the bowl and the yolks into the blender with
    1 cup milk
Turn blender on and add:
    1½ cups corn meal
    ½ cup oil
Beat egg whites stiff until they hold a peak. Sprinkle 1 tablespoon baking powder over them. Beat until creamy.

Pour blender corn mixture over egg whites and fold

57

in. Pour into 8″ x 8″ pyrex pan and bake at 350° until bottom is nice and brown.

This 2-step corn cake gets a little higher and finer textured than the quick one.

MIX-ME-QUICK CORN GRIDDLE CAKES

    3 eggs
    1 cup milk

Turn blender on and add in the order given.

    1 cup corn flour (unsifted)
    ½ cup oil
    1 tablespoon baking powder

Bake on hot griddle or pan in a little butter. These are light and golden and my kids really go for them. Stir every time you pour some to stir up the corn that might settle.

CORN WAFFLES

Same recipe as above only separate the eggs. Yolks in blender and whites in a mixing bowl. While the blender is mixing the corn flour, beat the egg whites stiff and add the baking powder to them after they are stiff. Beat creamy and pour the blender mixture over and fold in.

Farmers know the feeding value in corn. But do they know about it for themselves? If you want to learn anything about nutrition, read any farm magazine. Of course that's only for the benefit of the animals. When the farmer comes in the house to eat, his diet is centered around many, many, white flour products. White rice, white this and white that. Or else it gets peeled, or cooked, or fried to disgrace. These same practices he never would allow out in the farmyard because there he knows a little about nutrition.

CORN NOODLES

Look under Noodles to make corn noodles. Make a noodle ball and keep one in your refrigerator. When it is cold it will slice very thin. Slice whenever you want to add noodles quickly to something.

CORN NOODLE SACS

Roll out noodle dough. Rolling only one way works the best. Corn is the hardest to work with of the grains, because it's the grainiest. But this rolls well. Roll it on arrowroot flour. When you have about a 6- or 7-inch piece rolled out, lay a jar cover (any cover about 5 inches across) on top and cut out a large circle.

Fill half of it with raw hamburger and a little chopped onion. Season and fold over the empty half. Seal the edges tight and brown in a little oil or cook in a broth. Crumble the meat loosely so it will cook through better, and don't put in too much.

POPCORN FLOUR

To make popcorn flour, pop popcorn with as much oil as popcorn. This adds the shortening to the cookies. However, they are good made with dry popcorn too. Fill the blender with popcorn. Let it whiz and push popcorn down with a wooden spoon until it's all caught in and blended good. This takes a little practice. You can sift it through the flour sifter if you like. It's easier to handle made with oil because it doesn't get so powdery while you're blending and produce a miniature snow storm in the kitchen.

ANGEL FOOD COOKIES

6 egg whites
4 tablespoons honey
2 cups popcorn flour
1 teaspoon pure vanilla

Put egg whites and honey in top of double boiler. Beat until light and fluffy over boiling water. Add vanilla. Fold in popcorn flour and drop by spoonfuls on heavily buttered pan, so they don't stick.

This was published in *Prevention*, September, 1965. Now I have a few more ideas to add to my first one. Keep this flour on hand. It is cheap and good.

POPCORN MAGIC MIX COOKIES

Make one batch of Magic Mix. Add 1 tablespoon baking powder. Pour into a bowl and add 6 cups of popcorn flour, or as heavy as you want to make the dough. Drop on buttered cookie sheet and bake at 350° until browned.

The customer demands, "Where's the manager? I can't eat this steak!"

The waitress replies, "Why call him? He can't eat it either."

POPCORN PANCAKES

    3 eggs
    1 cup milk
    3 cups popcorn flour or until it's thick
    ½ cup oil
    1 tablespoon baking powder
Blend all together. Help mix in baking powder with spoon if the mixture thickens too fast after you add it. Bake on griddle or in butter in pan. These have a good flavor but a little different texture.

POPCORN CANDY

Here you can be as versatile as it is possible to be. Here are some of the ways I mixed popcorn flour to make little candies, and they all were good. I'm sure that there will be a lot of ideas to come concerning popcorn flour.

2 parts peanut butter
1 part honey
popcorn flour

Mix in the flour until it's stiff and form into a roll or little balls.

Butterscotch

Blend one cup of cut up dates with ½ cup hot water. Turn on and off to chop the dates. Don't blend them fine. Leave some of the dates in pieces, so they will be in the candy. Add nuts or whatever you want, or leave plain. Stir in popcorn flour and drop by spoonfuls into popcorn flour to coat them. Roll in to coat them and put on plate.

Butter

Mix equal parts of honey and butter. Add vanilla, then mix in enough flour to stiffen. Form into little balls.

Molasses

Add a little honey to the molasses to sweeten it enough. Stir in flour to stiffen.

Natural Fruit Flavors

Mix with any raw fruit jelly you have until stiff. They are especially good with grape.

If they are sticky, roll them in flour. They are attractive coated with this white popcorn flour. Or, mix in enough to make them good and stiff. Make both kinds for variety.

CRANBERRY RELISH OR JAM

This cranberry relish or jell is different. Boil slowly 1 cup honey with one box of pectin powder. Add ½ cup of whole cranberries and boil slowly for about 10 minutes. Chop up 1½ cups raw cranberries in the blender and add to the surejell after it has boiled. Chill.

This makes a good jelly for using up any chopped fruit. Good with sour cherries too. Good with meat.

QUICK CRANBERRY RELISH

Chop one package cranberries in a can of thawed orange juice in blender. Add honey to sweeten.

CRANBERRY-RASPBERRY GELATIN

Cook one cup of cranberries in one cup of water until their skins crack. Meanwhile soften 1 tablespoon of gelatin in a little cold water. When the cranberries have popped, take them off the stove and add the gelatin. Stir to melt it in, then add ½ cup of honey. Stir in one box of frozen raspberries. Chop one cup of cranberries in the blender and add. Let set. Frozen cranberries chop very well in the blender.

Variations: Add grapes cut in half, pineapple, nuts, marshmallows, or apple pieces. Add one alone or any in combination.

DAIRY PRODUCTS

Part of the year we have milk, when Mrs. Cow chooses to provide some. I make butter, cheese cakes and pizza pies in the blender.

You can use dairy milk, sweet or sour, or buttermilk in any of the baked products, or recipes asking for milk in this book.

MAKING BUTTER +

Run the milk through a separator or skim the cream off the top of the milk. After it has been chilled or refrigerated a day or so the cream rises to the top. Let the cream stand in the refrigerator a day. This makes it thick and heavy. The cream should have aged a little to make the best butter. Put in the blender and blend. If the cream is rich it will be butter almost immediately. You will see it turn into a sandy-like texture. Take a rubber spatula or wooden spoon and help form it into a lump on the top while the blender is running on low. Or stop the blender and stir or push it into a lump by hand. Pour off the buttermilk. Put the butter in a bowl and with a rubber scraper keep working it under running cold water until the water is clear or change water until you have the buttermilk all worked out. Use either a rubber scraper or wooden spoon to make working with butter easier. After you make butter a few times you can make it in a few minutes. The butter changes colors with the seasons because of what the cow eats.

COTTAGE CHEESE

There might be some of you who are new at making cottage cheese. Let the milk sour. If you can let it sour right in the kettle it makes less work. When it is thick set it on medium heat and let it heat through. It must heat through to the top. You might have to stir it, but do so very gently. However it must not reach a boil or get too hot. The hotter it gets the harder the curd. It doesn't hurt if you have overheated it if you are using the cheese in the blender. It's only if you want to eat it at the table that you want to keep it tender. Set it off the heat and let it cool. Pour into a cloth or wire strainer and let it drain.

CHEESE CHIP DIPS

Put cottage cheese in the blender. Turn on. Add milk until it's smooth. Pour into a dish and add a dry soup mix and little pieces of meat or green and red vegetables. Add seasoning to taste.

CHEESE CAKE

Since home-made cottage cheese varies in dryness, I'll give you the method instead of precise recipes.

Fill blender about half full with cottage cheese and turn on. Add milk until it's nice and smooth. Now to make it stiff when it's cold, add either one-half cup of melted butter to the running blender or a teaspoon of gelatin melted in a little hot milk. Add honey and vanilla and almond flavorings to taste. It doesn't take much honey because milk has a natural sweetness.

Variations for above

Drain a can of crushed pineapple or your own canned pineapple. Use the juice for blending the cheese and stir the pineapple into the batter. Pour into pyrex pan and chill. Or stiffen a can of crushed pineapple with a teaspoon of gelatin. Set a layer of this on the bottom or top of the cheesecake.

Pour on a crumb crust. Top with cinnamon.

Top with a gelatin made with strawberries and pineapple. Use a tablespoon of gelatin to a pint of fruit. Heat the pineapple juice and add the softened gelatin to it to melt. Stir the strawberries in raw. Sweeten to taste. Pour on cheese cake and let set.

Make any of these in a crumb crust or leave them plain. They all freeze well.

To the crumb crust add butter, cinnamon, or both.

PIZZA

2 cups of tomatoes (canned or raw, blended)
1 cup dry cottage cheese
1 very full tablespoon honey
1 teaspoon vinegar
1 small clove of garlic, or a larger clove cut in half
Blend until smooth. Spread on your favorite crust or on the following Quick Crust.

Spread tiny meat balls over the crust (raw or cooked). Sprinkle with seasoning salt. Pour the sauce over the crust and sprinkle that heavily with oregano flakes. Bake at 350°.

Variations: Leave out the honey and vinegar. It's good plain too. Omit the garlic and sprinkle chopped onion over the meat. Use any meat or sausage you want. You may also use any vegetable, olives, anchovies, etc.

This pizza is cheap, fast and easy to make, and rivals the taste of any. The more sour the cottage cheese, the closer it tastes like the real thing.

QUICK CRUST

    3 eggs
    1 cup milk (warm)
    1 tablespoon dry yeast or one cake yeast
    1½ cups oat and rice flours mixed
    ½ cup oil
    1 tablespoon baking powder

Blend the eggs and the milk. Take the cover off and add ingredients in the order given. Pour into a buttered pan and spread out thin. It will be thin but until you have the tomato sauce blended it sets enough that you can lay the meat on it. This blender-full of crust makes enough for two batches of the above sauce.

DAIRY ICE CREAM AND SHAKES

GOOD OLD HOME MADE ICE CREAM

When our cow is milking, we like to enjoy a freezer ice cream. Hand cranking the ice cream makes it a real reward when that freezer can finally be opened. This is my recipe that I have never shared yet with anyone till now. We made a lot of ice cream until we had it just as we wanted it.

Set the freezer can into a big enough kettle to let water boil around it. In other words, you are creating a double boiler. Set this on high heat.

In blender:
    8 eggs
    3 tablespoons gelatin
      some of the milk to blend it smooth
In freezer can:
    ½ gallon milk (whole)
    2¾ cups light raw sugar

66

Later add:

    1 quart cream
    3 tablespoons pure vanilla
    1 teaspoon pure almond

Heat over the boiling water until hot and sugar is melted. Pour the blended eggs into the can and stir until the whole mixture is hot. Keep one hand on the side of the can at the top level of the milk. When it's all so hot you can't stand your hand there, take the can out and add one quart of cream and the flavorings. Freeze. Makes one gallon and a half.

For butterscotch use dark raw sugar and no flavorings.

For mocha use dark raw sugar, a little less milk and add strong coffee to suit your taste. No flavorings.

If you like richness, increase the cream; if not, increase the milk. Cream richness will vary.

KIDS' PLEASER ICE CREAM

Make any of the ice cream recipes in this book. Leave out all the milk or most of it. Go outside where there is some nice clean snow. Stir in snow until it looks like ice cream. Watch for the first heavy snowfall without wind. There usually is at least one such snowfall every winter. If your car was outside and is heavy with snow, use that off the top, not taking it off way to the metal. This is something for the kids to remember.

FOR BLENDER MILK SHAKES
OR ICE CREAM

Cook any ice cream recipe, without the milk, and keep this in the refrigerator. Freeze the milk part in ice cubes. When you want a milk shake, take a gob of the cooked mixture, put it in the blender, and add milk cubes while blending until it is ice cream. Let the milk cubes thaw a little bit before blending. It becomes routine to keep milk cubes along with ice cubes. Add 3 tablespoons carob per blender for carob milk shakes.

The milk cubes can be any milk—dairy, magic, sesame, sunflower, or other.

SNOW ICE CREAM
(An Unusual Treat)

In top of large double boiler (or make a large one by setting a kettle or large pyrex bowl in a large kettle with water in it):

    1 cup of cold water
    1 tablespoon gelatin

Turn on burner and let gelatin melt in. Add:

    1½ cups of turbinado sugar. Let melt in.

In blender:

    6 eggs, blend and slowly add while running:
    2 cups of dry milk
    1 cup of oil (soybean is good)

This is quite thick. Add slowly to hot mixture in double boiler, stirring hard with a wire whip. As soon as it's hot and very smooth, take off hot water at once. Let get hot, but do not overcook. Add about 2 tablespoons vanilla and about ¼ teaspoon almond (just a touch, not too much).

Let cool. Then add snow until it's very thick as ice cream. The colder it is, of course, the thicker and richer you will have it. Snow can be added while it is still warm, if they absolutely can't wait. But it will be thinner and less rich. This makes about a gallon finished product—enough for 6 people to make pigs of themselves, or enough for a crowd for dessert.

GELATINS

Here is where you can really create. Gelatin and the blender go hand in hand. The blender can do things with gelatins that nothing else can. Keep your food wholesome and use fruits and fruit juices instead of the artificially flavored and colored stuff. If some of us knew what these substances are, we would never think of eating them. Instead order gelatin by the pound. I buy it in 10-pound lots at a time. This stores and keeps well on your shelf. Gelatin, we all know, is a beneficial food. Put that together with a raw fruit or juice and you have spent your time wisely. If you are making it in the conventional way, first soak the gelatin with a little cold water to soften it; then add as little hot water as possible to melt it. Now add your raw fruits and juices to this and mix it up. If you do use the juice to heat the gelatin, use only part of it so you can still add most of it raw. This goes for all except pineapple which cannot be used raw as it won't stiffen because of an enzyme action.

FLUFFING GELATINS

Any gelatin can be fluffed up in the blender once it has set. It will thin-fluff and thicken again when it's poured back into the bowl. The gelatin should be made a little heavier than the normal tablespoon to a pint recipe. Fluffing it changes the appearance and taste. It would seem as though whipped cream was blended in, although you didn't add anything.

69

INSTANT GELATIN DESSERTS

There are three degrees of making instant gelatins stiff in the blender.

1 tablespoon to a blender—gives a two-layered effect clear on the bottom

2 tablespoons to a blender, whipped

3 tablespoons to a blender, whipped and stiff

1 can of frozen juice or 1 package fruit to a blender

Put one cup of warm to hot water in the blender. While it is running add the dry gelatin. Turn to high and let blend until high, white and foamy. Add the can of frozen juice or fruit. It will thicken immediately. If you want to use it right away at the table, use 3 tablespoons of gelatin. To set cold and have a softer gelatin use 1 or 2 tablespoons. If you want a clear gelatin, follow directions for making it the conventional way of soaking it first. Use any fresh frozen fruit of your own, frozen fruit purees of your own, or buy frozen grape, orange or fruit juice. Also you can use frozen berries such as strawberries, raspberries, blueberries, or whatever is available in your area.

BOTTLED FRUIT JUICES

To make quick gelatins from bottle or fresh juice, blend amount of gelatin required with one cup of fruit juice. Blend long until it's melted and blended in. Add the rest of the juice and ice cubes, and blend until thick. The more gelatin you use, the faster it will thicken.

Hint: If you are using ice cubes to set your gelatin in the blender, be sure they are blended in well. It won't matter if you eat it right away, but if it's kept for a while the ice crystals or pieces will melt and leave a watery hole in the gelatin.

WHITE MARSHMELLOS FOR GELATINS

Put one cup hot water in blender and add 2 table-spoons gelatin. Let foam up and melt in. Add ½ cup honey, ½ cup oil, and vanilla to taste. Now drop in ice cubes until it is thick and can't take any more. Drop by spoonfuls on set gelatin or into soft gelatin.

WHITE MARSHMELLO TOPPING
FOR GELATIN

Put one cup warm water in the blender and add 1 ta-blespoon gelatin. Let it foam up good and add ½ cup oil, ½ cup honey, vanilla or vanilla and almond to taste. Add three ice cubes one by one until blended in. Pour over gelatin. Let set. This can be used on top of a gela-tin or between layers.

SUNFLOWER MARSHMELLO

Same as marshmellos but add one cup sunflower seeds to beginning mixture and let them blend until smooth.

THREE-LAYERED PURPLE

First layer: Put one cup warm to hot water in the blender. While it is running add 2 tablespoons gelatin. Let foam up high and melt in. Add one can of frozen grape juice. Blend in. Pour into clear pyrex cake pan. Set cold to stiffen while you make next layer.

Second layer: Put one cup warm to hot water in the blender. Add one tablespoon gelatin. Blend until high and foamy. Add one can grape juice. Pour over first layer. This layer will separate: the bottom will be clear jello and the top will be fluffed. Now finish it off with a layer of marshmello topping.

FLOWER POT GELATIN
(name my youngest boy gave it)
ORANGE—WHITE—RED

Put the one cup of warm water in blender. Add 2 tablespoons gelatin. Let blend until high and foamy. Add:

1 can frozen orange juice
2 tablespoons honey

Blend, set cold to stiffen in clear pyrex cake pan. Make marshmellos for gelatin next. Drop by spoonfuls over the set orange gelatin. Make clear raspberry gelatin next and pour around and between the marshmellos. Let set. It is pretty.

CLEAR RASPBERRY

Soften 1 tablespoon gelatin in a little cold water. Add 1 cup very hot water and melt it. Stir in one package of partly thawed or thawed raspberries.

GELATIN GAIETY

Now you have an idea what you can do. Set out what you have in the freezer or cupboard. Mix and alternate layers for colors and effects. They turn out so many different ways. If the pan is warm chances are that the bottom layer will be half clear. No matter how it gets they are always attractive. For a picnic make them with three tablespoons gelatin to keep them stiff.

Hint: Putting pan in freezer to get cold while making gelatin makes it set even faster.

IDEAS FOR COMBINATIONS

Orange and canned pineapple.

Grape and blueberry. Mix some blueberries in the gelatin. Keep some back for topping. Melt 1 teaspoon gelatin to a pint of blueberries and the liquid they have. Set the gelatin in a crumb crust and spoon the rest of the blueberries over the top when serving. The colors are something!

Pineapple with any flavor.

Bananas with any flavor.

Apricot puree.

Orange with thinly sliced oranges.

Peach puree.

Use whatever fruit you may have in your area and create your own combinations. They are good poured into a crumb crust for a pie.

FRUIT MARSHMELLO CANDY

Put one cup warm water in blender. Let blend with 3 tablespoons gelatin until high and foamy. Add ½ cup corn oil, vanilla to taste, 3 or 4 tablespoons honey and frozen juice or berries.

Pink Raspberry

Make basic recipe above. Add box of frozen raspberries. This thickens fast. Keep blending and helping with spatula. Stiff gelatin mixtures become liquid again in the blender and will set fast after they are poured out. Drop by spoonfuls on plate. If raspberries are already sweetened omit the honey and vanilla. Almond flavor can be added.

Pale Pink Strawberry

Follow same instructions as for raspberry using strawberry as the fruit.

Purple Grape

Add can of frozen grape juice. Omit honey and vanilla. Pour into pan and cut in squares.

Orange

Add can of frozen grape juice. Omit honey and vanilla. Pour into pan.

Peanut

Make basic recipe. Add a cup or two of chopped peanuts. Peanut butter may be used for a stronger flavor. Without peanut butter it stays nice and white. Pour into pan.

These all can be rolled in arrowroot flour if wanted. They are more of a confection than a gelatin. If you make all of these you really have a colorful selection.

The longer you whip gelatins in the blender the more they will whip up—to a certain point of course. Let these set at room temperature. These can be cut up and frozen as they freeze well. Thaw completely before serving.

FRESH OR DRIED FRUIT WHIPS

    1 cup warm water
    1 tablespoon gelatin
Blend and add after white and foamy:
    ½ cup oil
    ½ cup honey
    1 cup fruit
      or
    1 package frozen fruit partly thawed
    2 egg whites, beaten very stiff in bowl
Pour the blender mixture over the egg whites and fold in. Ready to serve or chill and serve.

Variations: Strawberries, raspberries, cranberries. Dried fruits—prunes, raisins, figs, apricots with almond flavoring. If using dried fruits, put the fruit in all at once. Turn the blender on and off to chop it first, then blend. This makes it easier on the blender. Chop on low first, Mr. Nusz says. Do not blend too smooth—leave flecks of fruit in whip.

VANILLA WHIP

Use 3 eggs; separate the whites into a bowl. Cook the yolks in one cup of water. Put into the blender, add the gelatin, and continue the recipe as above. Add vanilla alone or with almond flavorings instead of fruit. This can be used as a topping for other desserts too in place of whipped cream or topping.

The dried fruit whips get a little stiffer when chilled because they have no liquid. These whips can be molded. A mousse is one of the above whips frozen. Vanilla whip frozen is near ice cream.

RAW FRUIT JAMS AND PUREES

We pick wild fruit in my father's and brother's hills and river-bottom land. These I make into purees in the blender which in turn, during the winter, are made into raw jellies, gelatins, drinks and punches. This wild fruit doesn't look like much, but oh the flavor hidden in them! The flavor is something! The color is beautiful and stays that way. I suppose tame gooseberry would be much the same.

MAKING FRUIT PUREE

If you were eating the fruit while you were picking it, it shouldn't be any dirtier in the house. It can be put straight into the blender. Fill blender with fruit. Add one cup of honey. Turn on and off to pull the fruit down. Blend until smooth and strain through a medium large wire strainer. If you have the finer one it will let the puree through but hold back the seeds and peelings. NOW: don't throw away those peelings and seeds. Put them in a jar, add some water, let set overnight, and you have a juice to drink for breakfast. This works with any dark fruit such as grapes, chokecherries, cherries and gooseberries. I'm sure it will work with the fruit native to your area too. Also use tame fruits. Should you forget a jar of juice for some time, it turns into a wine that can be tolerated too.

Put these purees into freezer containers and freeze. They don't freeze too hard, so some fruits can be used for jelly just like that, or as a topping for ice creams, etc. The red, purple and dark fruits are very good this way. Fruits that discolor, such as apples, pears, etc., might need some ascorbic acid added. They don't do as well as the red and dark fruit.

RAW JELLIES

Mix one pound fruit puree, or approximately one pound whole fruit or one can frozen grape juice with one box of a pectin jell. (There's more in one brand than in the other.) Add honey to sweeten. Blend together or stir hard. In a couple of hours it will be thick. This gets real thick the longer it sets. For a thinner jelly add more puree.

RAW WHOLE STRAWBERRY JELL

Thaw the frozen strawberries or whatever berry fruit you have. Mix the juice with the pectin and cook, simmering it well for about 5 minutes with 1 cup of honey. Add the fruit whole and set aside to thicken.

Method No. 2

Cook one cup of honey with 1 box of pectin until thick and bubbly. Take off the stove and add the whole fruit or puree.

76

Method No. 3

Mash part of the fruit and cook with the pectin. Add the rest of the fruit whole or raw. Let set to thicken.

CONCORD GRAPES

I realize that if you have to do all your food shopping in a city, you might not be able to obtain much more than concord grapes in red or dark fruits. These are in season late in the summer and really make up into good eating and drinking.

Put one cup of honey in the blender. Add 4½ cups of de-stemmed grapes. Blend well and strain through wire strainer, stirring to keep it straining. Freeze this *strained concentrate* for winter use in jelly, drinks, gelatins or punches. Don't try to strain too much out of the seeds and pulp, because if you put what's left in the strainer into a glass jar and add water, it will make a good breakfast juice. Keep in the refrigerator overnight or longer before using. Pour through the strainer before serving. This will surprise you how strong the flavor gets. It's possible to add water to the pulp again and still get another drink. I usually pour enough off the top for breakfast and add more water for another time. Add more honey if needed.

CONCORD GRAPE JELLY

Put one cup of above grape concentrate in a saucepan and set on burner on medium heat. Let come to a boil and stir in 3 boxes of pectin. This cooks thick so watch for scorching. When good and thick, put in blender and add about 4 cups of the raw concentrate. Blend and add more honey if needed. Refrigerate. This method gives more of the cooked texture to the jelly but still keeps most of the jelly raw. If you have a thick crystallized honey, it helps make the jelly thicker too because it will do its part to re-thicken after the jelly is refrigerated.

"SPOTS"
(Candy)

Something unusual children will get a kick out of.
In blender:

1 box pectin
1 cup boiling water

Blend until thick and glossy. Add one small can of unthawed frozen grape juice. Blend well. Drop by ½ teaspoonful on wax paper on cookie sheet, or in a pyrex cake pan to form spots. These are thin so set away carefully in a dry place for a couple of days or until they set and can be lifted off. Serve on a colored platter. For strips or cutouts, pour enough in a pyrex cake pan to cover the bottom. Put away to set; when completely set, cut in long strips or cut out with cookie cutters into different shapes.

These are easy to handle after they are set. The only thing is to let them alone until they ARE set. Numbers or other ideas could be cut out to use on birthdays, anniversaries, etc.

Syrup Using Spot Recipe

The spots recipe makes a good pancake or topping syrup, stays syrupy and will not jell. Also is tasty spread on jelly roll, and makes an attractive looking jelly roll.

GRAPE FLUFF

Cook one cup water, 1 cup honey, and 2 packages pectin for a few minutes. When it looks good and syrupy, put one can of frozen grape juice in the blender. Pour on the pectin syrup and blend until fluffy. Juice has to be frozen. Pour into bowl or jar.

78

MUFFINS

Make muffins with any of the flours or mixture of flours—corn, rice, oats, soybean, and the Millyun Dollar Mix everyone likes. Buckwheat has a different flavor when used alone. It's not too bad, but some people might not like it. Soybean is real good in these recipes.

If I were to name every muffin by name that can be made with these recipes they would fill the book alone. So besides each of the different flours, you can vary these with all the dried fruits, nuts, seeds, blueberries, chopped cranberry, cherry, cinnamon, spices and of course fresh fruit, such as apple pieces added to the dough before baking.

Sweet Muffins

If you don't want to eat your muffins with jam or jell, you might want to sweeten them. Add ½ cup honey and fruits and nuts or use one of the variations above. Use the muffin peaks for these.

These muffins are all made by the 2-step method, but can be made entirely in the blender if you are in a hurry. Another shortcut is to pour them into a buttered cake pan and cut into squares.

Bake all muffins at 350°.

MUFFINS

    3 eggs, separated—whites into a bowl, yolks into
      blender
    1 cup milk
    1 cup your choice flour (unsifted)
    ½ cup oil

Add to the running blender in the order given. Beat the egg whites very stiff. Add 1 tablespoon baking powder and beat until high and creamy. Put blender mixture over egg whites and fold in. Pour into buttered cup cake pans. Bake.

These are light and fluffy textured. They are crinkly and shiny on the top. Most of them cool with a slight depression on top. Just right to put in butter, jell, or honey. Umm!

MUFFIN PEAKS

For a muffin with more body and one that rises to a peak in the middle, use the same recipe as above, only add 1½ cups of either of the flours.

SOYBEAN SOFTIES

Make these when you want something special. There is no trace of the soybean flavor in them when done. Soybean gets heavier in the mixture. Help along on the top of the blender if necessary.

  3 eggs separated—whites in bowl, yolks in blender
 1½ cups milk
Start blender and while running add:
 1 cup soybean flour (unsifted)
 ½ cup oil
Beat egg whites stiff and sprinkle 1 tablespoon baking powder over them. Beat until high and creamy. Fold in blender mixture. Bake.

For a heavier soybean muffin, omit ½ cup milk.

These soybean softies are light, airy, and are a beautiful, golden brown. Fill depression with favorites such as butter, jelly, peanut butter, honey, etc. Attractive!

NOODLES

With the use of gelatin, you get a resilient dough that can be used to make noodles with any flour. With the rolling pin it is possible to roll out any dough very thin. They can also be made in a noodle machine. If you have ever made noodles in a noodle machine, you know that the dough has to be just right. Run it through the widest setting a few times first until it comes out smooth. Then lay it away to dry a bit and start on another piece. Keep alternating and drying in between rolling them thinner. Work with small pieces. Stop at about the second last thinness.

In blender:

Blend 3 eggs

In bowl:

    1 cup your choice flour or mixture (unsifted)
    3 tablespoons plain dry gelatin
      mix well

Stir in the eggs and keep stirring. It will get thicker as the gelatin softens. Use a rubber scraper to form it into a ball. This noodle ball can be put into the refrigerator and sliced very thin for quick noodles. It sets very hard and is easy to slice with a sharp knife.

For noodles right away, roll the ball in arrowroot flour. Divide it into 4 pieces. Roll out each piece on arrowroot flour or use the machine. Cut into strips. For noodle sacs, cut into squares or circles, fill one-half with a little hamburger and fold the empty half over and seal. Brown in a little oil or cook in a broth or soup. For making any of these, I prefer rolling them out by hand on a cutting board. For almost no work at all, slice them off a noodle ball.

81

NUTS, SEEDS AND COCONUT

Have you ever been called nuts by anyone? That would be a real insult. But we are called nuts all the time, for that is what our name "Nusz" means in the German language from which we are descendants.

Now to start, buy whatever you can get: raw shelled pecans, walnuts, mixed nuts, raw peanuts, unsweetened coconut, sunflower seeds, pumpkin seeds, raw soybeans, whole buckwheat kernels, and the finer seeds like sesame and wheat germ. Some of these are only available at Christmas time in the grocery stores.

SUPERB PARTY MIX FOR NIBBLING

Mix whatever you have of the list except wheat germ or sesame. Put them in a baking pan and roast at 350° or 400° until nice and brown. While hot, sprinkle with your favorite seasoning such as vege-all. Add an equal amount of raw nuts and sunflower and pumpkin seeds. Add anything except raw soybeans or raw peanuts. Wheat germ and sesame are too fine for this. The soybeans are hard but good. Add broken pieces of chips from "party time." Warm before eating if desired.

GRINDING AND TOASTING NUTS

In the blender, grind any nuts or seeds to the consistency of corn meal. Put in different containers. Grind whole raw soybeans, unsweetened coconut, raw peanuts, walnuts, pecans, or any nuts you have, or seeds such as pumpkin, millet, sunflower.

In a frying pan such as a copper bottom stainless steel, put 2 cups of either ground soybeans, ground peanuts, walnuts, millet, or ground nuts of any kind. Toast on medium heat turning all the while with a spoon. At first it takes quite a while, but when it starts browning it will brown fast. Toast until a light brown color.

Keep on hand both raw and toasted peanuts, all nuts, coconut, wheat germ, and millet. Soybeans are almost impossible to use raw because of the flavor they have.

You are now ready to make quite a display of cookies and candies. Mix the toasted and the raw ground seeds because when using all raw, the taste just isn't right. With ground soybeans use only the toasted.

WHEAT GERM CRISPS

To one cup of Magic Mix add 1 teaspoon baking powder, ⅓ cup toasted wheat germ, and ⅔ cup raw wheat germ. Mix well and drop on buttered cookie sheet. They spread out during baking into a crisp cookie.

MILLET CRISPS

Use ground millet, part toasted, the same as wheat germ.

WHEAT GERM BARS

Make Magic Mix with only the egg yolks. Beat the egg whites stiff. Add 1 tablespoon baking powder, and beat creamy. Fold 1 cup toasted wheat germ and 1½ cups raw wheat germ into the egg whites, with the Magic Mix. Pour into an 11½" x 17" buttered cookie pan. Bake at 350°. When done cut into bars. This has a cake-like texture.

WALNUT, PEANUT, PECAN, OR
ANY GROUND NUT CRISPS

    1 cup Magic Mix
    1 cup ground walnuts (or other)
    1 cup toasted ground walnuts
    1 teaspoon baking powder
Drop on buttered cookie sheet and bake at 325°-350°.

Millet has a little different flavor, and is fine if you like millet.

These crisps are good using nuts and seeds for flour.

SOYBEAN CEREAL

Grind the raw soybeans in the blender. Set frying pan on the stove to get hot while they are blending. When blended as fine as you want your cereal, pour into hot frying pan. Turn heat to medium and stir steadily to brown or toast the cereal. When the cereal is a nice light brown color, add water to equal the cereal. Turn heat on low, cover and let steam while you make the rest of the breakfast. Add more water if it gets too dry. Eat as you would any cereal. Vary it by adding fruits such as raisins. If you have whole grain of any kind, you can use this same method, although other grains are good without toasting. Soybean is good toasted, but the raw flavor is too strong.

If there's any of this cereal left make Soybean Cookies (next recipe).

SOYBEAN COOKIES

Use leftover Soybean Cereal. Add sunflower seeds, dried fruits, ground nuts, ground toasted peanuts, coconut or what you have. Add 1 teaspoon baking powder for every cup you put in the mixing bowl. Mix with Magic Mix until well moistened. Stir hard to thicken. Bake. Very tasty. Serve these for tomorrow's breakfast. Add cut-up dates or raisins to sweeten them more. Or blend some into the Magic Mix before adding it to the cereal.

SUNFLOWER SEED MILK

1 cup seeds
1 cup hot water

Blend until smooth. Add water as it thickens, always blending until smooth. Thin slowly with 2 cups water, or as you want it.

For sunflower seed Magic Milk, add 3 eggs, (cooked) and thin to 4 to 5 cups.

GOODIE CUBES

To Sunflower Seed Milk, add honey and vanilla to taste, either one. If your kids enjoy eating ice cubes, they'll enjoy eating these. Freeze in ice cube trays. To use goodie cubes see next recipes.

INSTANT PUDDING

1 cup warm water
3 tablespoons gelatin

Blend well until white and foamy and gelatin is melted in. Add:

2 eggs (raw or cooked)
3 rounded tablespoons honey
1 teaspoon vanilla

While blender is running add:

3 tablespoons carob
½ cup oil

Now add Sunflower Seed Milk cubes until thick and high. If you are adding Goodie Cubes omit the honey and vanilla. Should any gelatin mixture in the blender get too thick and you still want to add more, keep working it under with the rubber scraper. It will thin again with time. If it seems just impossible to get it thinner, add a little liquid. When you pour this into a bowl it will thicken fast. Help along on the top by mixing it well to keep the ice going to the bottom. I make these instant gelatin puddings and milk shakes all summer long. I usually make them while they are washing up for dinner.

ANOTHER INSTANT PUDDING
(with ice)

1 cup warm water blended with 3 tablespoons gelatin

½ cup sunflower seeds

Keep adding water as it thickens until it is nice and smooth.

2 eggs

3 tablespoons honey

vanilla

3 tablespoons carob

½ cup oil

Add all ingredients while blender is running. Now add ice cubes until high and thick. These puddings are nice in a mold. Chill to mold.

INSTANT MILK SHAKES

Follow same recipes as the puddings omitting the gelatin. Add the ice cubes until thick like ice cream.

MILK

Any milk, dairy or dairyless, will fit into these recipes. It becomes a simple routine to have these cubes on hand all the time and when someone is hungry fill them up fast.

SUNFLOWER SEED SMOOTH PUDDING

    1 cup hot water
    1 tablespoon gelatin
Blend until white and add:
    1 cup sunflower seeds
Blend until thick. Keep adding water gradually until 1 cup is used up.

    3 eggs, raw or cooked
    ½ cup honey
    1 tablespoon vanilla
    ¼ teaspoon almond
    ¼ cup oil
Cool to set. After it is set, it will be just like cooked pudding at room temperature.

CAROB SMOOTH PUDDING

Add 3 tablespoons carob to above.

NUTTLES

    1 egg
    1 cup dates or raisins
    1 cup nut meats
Turn blender on and off until the egg and fruit are chopped and partly blended. Stir the mixture in a bowl with 1 cup of large nut meats. Spread in well-oiled pie plate. Bake until light brown. Break up into pieces and put in the candy dish. The date nuttle is the best tasting. Sprinkle some of them with cinnamon.

SEED AND NUT BUTTERS

Put a cupful of your favorite nuts or nut mix, seeds, such as sesame, sunflower seeds or pumpkin seeds or mix any combination in blender. Blend as fine as you can. Then add oil gradually until you get the consistency you want. To improve the flavor, toast some of the ground seeds or nuts in a frying pan and add the rest raw. Nuts and seeds can be toasted in the oven or pan.

MARSHMELLO NUT

Make Marshmellos (see Confections). Let them harden at room temperature. They stay softer this way. Roll them in toasted ground nuts, wheat germ, seeds, or soybeans.

SEEDMELLOS

Make Marshmellos or Marshmello Topping. While soft divide in different batches and mix with any of the toasted ground seeds, or nuts, adding part raw, or all ground raw. Drop by spoonfuls to set.

For using ground soybeans, toast all soybeans after you grind them. They will soften when mixed with the marshmello. I'm sure everyone will like the flavor of toasted soybeans.

For more Seed Candies look in the Confection section.

NUT BRITTLES

Make Magic Mix with double honey for soybean, coconut, whole buckwheat groats, and sunflower seeds. These seem to need more sweetness. These get crisp, brittle and sweet. They are more like a candy than a cookie.

SUNFLOWER SEED BRITTLE

Put one cup double honey Magic Mix back into the blender. Add two cups sunflower seeds and turn on and off to chop them. Don't chop them too fine so some will stay whole. Add 1 teaspoon baking powder and turn blender on and off to mix it in. Pour into buttered cookie pan and bake at 325° to 350°. Break into pieces when done.

SOYBEAN OR BUCKWHEAT
GROATS BRITTLE

1 cup whole buckwheat
    or
1 cup ground toasted soybeans
1 cup Magic Mix
1 teaspoon baking powder

Mix, pour in buttered pan and bake. The buckwheat groats are chewy and tasty. Make these nut crisps and brittles of one nut or seed alone or mix them.

COCONUT BRITTLE
(unsweetened coconut)

Make the same way as sunflower brittle.

PANCAKES

With the blender pancakes are fast and easy. For all-white pancakes use rice and oat flours. Buckwheat can be used alone, but is best when mixed in with the other flours. Millyun Dollar Mix is good. For corn and popcorn pancakes see Corn. These recipes are good with any flour mixture. The milk used can be a Magic, sour, dairy, or buttermilk. Or even water may be used. If water is used, use very full cup of unsifted flour.

FEATHER-LITE QUICK PANCAKES

3 eggs
1 cup Magic Milk (or any milk)
1 cup oat or rice flour (or your choice), unsifted
½ cup oil
1 tablespoon baking powder

3 Leaping TBSP MPS POWDER

89

Add in the order given. Use one flour alone, or mix any amount of different kinds together. Bake in butter in pan, or on hot griddle. If you are using a griddle use butter for the first time. They won't stick after that. There's nothing like butter to grease a griddle or waffle iron, and keep it from sticking. This does not mean margarine, only pure butter.

FIRMER PANCAKES

For a pancake more like the packaged mixes you buy, use this recipe.

4 eggs
1 cup milk
1½ cups flour
½ cup oil
1 tablespoon baking powder

Add in the order given. Turn on and off at the end to pull down baking powder. Let come to a stop then turn on fast to create a suction action. These recipes will rise to the top of the blender. Spoon directly into the pan and you will have only your blender to wash.

WAFFLES

For waffles or a different textured pancake, separate the eggs in the above recipe. Beat the egg whites stiff in a bowl. Add the baking powder to them when very stiff. Beat again until high and creamy. Pour the blender mixture over the whites and fold in. Use the yolks in the blender mixture. Bake the first waffles by brushing butter over the grids, top and bottom, and closing the iron for a few minutes to allow the butter to season the waffle iron. It won't stick after that. Soybean is good in waffles.

LARGER FLUFF RECIPE
(for pancakes or waffles or muffins)

6 eggs—whites in mixing bowl, yolks in blender
1 cup your choice milk
1½ cups your choice flour
¾ cup oil

Add in the order given. Beat the egg whites very stiff. Add 1 tablespoon baking powder to them and beat again until high and creamy. Pour the blender mixture over all at once and fold in. Use for pancakes, waffles, or bake in buttered muffin tins

Hint: Freeze waffles and reheat in a toaster. Use as a base for desserts, ice cream, etc. with a raw fruit syrup poured over all.

SYRUPS FOR PANCAKES OR DESSERTS

Serve pancakes with a pat of butter and one of the following syrups.

Dark Raw Sugar Syrup

Boil one part dark raw sugar to one part water. Simmer a while and serve hot. This is a heavy syrup. For a thinner syrup add more water.

Butter Syrup

Add butter to the above syrup and serve hot. A taste treat!

Fruit Juice Syrup

Boil and simmer 1 cup honey with one box apple pectin until thick and glossy. Add a bottle of pure fruit juice, or your frozen purees. A cup of fruit juice can be simmered along with the pectin. This will be thin but heavier bodied than just juice alone.

For a thicker fruit syrup, use 2 boxes of pectin. This

will even turn to jell if it lasts long enough. Always add the juice raw without cooking.

Variations: Add whole fruits such as fresh or frozen blueberries, mulberries, etc., raw to these syrups. Any combination seems to be good.

Some of the juices available in health catalogues and grocery departments are: black cherry, wild blackberry, red raspberry, grape. Add to that the purees that you can freeze in your locality. I have in my freezer wild gooseberry, choke cherry, wild grape, strawberries from the garden and sour cherries when I can get some.

PARTY TIME

Make nourishing chips for dipping or eating! There are so many ways and varieties you can make here that I'm almost at a loss how to start. You can make these in any shape that you want to cut them. They can be broken up and added to the Party Nut Mix. (See Nuts.) They can be used as crackers with or broken into soup, or cooked into the soup. Make the dough of any flour, all ground nuts, all sesame seeds or wheat germ. Roll in any seed or nuts on the top. Season with any flavor seasoning. This is the dough:

In bowl:

Mix three tablespoons dry plain gelatin with one cup of flour. Add 3 blended eggs and stir into the flour. Keep stirring until it thickens. The gelatin softens and thickens the dough. When thick form into a ball with a rubber scraper. Roll this ball in seeds. Make as many kinds of dough balls as you want of different flours. Roll each in a different seed. Now roll out with rolling pin, sprinkling on more seeds and rolling them into the dough. Sprinkle with seasoning salt; also sprinkle the cookie sheet heavily with seasoning salt to keep them from sticking to it. Cut into desired shapes and lay on seasoned cookie sheet. Bake until brown. All the flours are good except buckwheat alone has a strong flavor.

Seeds to roll in—sesame, wheat germ, poppy, sunflower, pumpkin.

WHEAT GERM

Make the dough using wheat germ for the flour. Roll in wheat germ.

ALL SESAME
(very good)

Make the dough using 1 cup sesame seeds for the flour. Roll in sesame seeds. Let stand a while to give it a chance to thicken.

NUT FLOURS

Make the dough of ground nuts, all raw or partly baked. Roll in nut pieces.

Seasoning is just for flavor. It isn't a necessity if you don't want it.

Cut into squares, strips, diamonds, etc.

PEAS

Have you ever shelled your peas and looked at that beautiful green mound of shells and thought "what a waste"? A large amount of shells and a little bowl of peas. Well, the shells taste every bit as good as the peas. They are sweet and the flavor is the same.

Here are four ways to eat or use these shells.

1. Set the blender jar beside you. Cut or tear the stem end off and pull the string down and off all in one operation. Throw the pods in the blender. Turn on and off and push down with the rubber scraper until they are mushed up. Strain through wire strainer and use juice for cooking the peas or other uses.

2. Set a waterless saucepan beside you. Throw the pods in as you shell. Add a little water and cover. Heat until steam starts escaping. Turn off and let set till burner is cool. They are steamed and nice and green. Empty saucepan, water and all, into blender. Blend and strain. Use as wanted. The flavor is better than the raw above.

3. Cut off the stem end as you shell them and pull the strings down the sides. Break each half pea pod in half the long way (to the inside). Peel off the green flesh. These pieces are good raw for snacking, raw in salads, or cooked with peas.

4. Throw them back in the garden for mulch.

PICKLES

My first interest in putting up cucumbers came, of course, after I was married. This process I learned from my mother-in-law, Mrs. Huldina Nusz. Here is her famous dill pickle recipe written by her in her own words.

⟶ DILL PICKLES

Pack half gallon jar with small or medium sized washed cucumbers. Pack solid. Then on top of cucumbers, add:

    1 heaping tablespoons salt (not iodized)
    1 teaspoon mixed pickling spices
      about 2 cloves garlic, cut up

Then add fist sized green dill. Add boiling water, then seal. Do not use softened or treated water.

Now, here is what I add to that to make mine. A fresh stick of horseradish root.

OUR FAVORITE PICKLES

Pack ½ gallon jar full of cucumbers. Add on the top:

2 tablespoons salt
2 tablespoons pickling spice
  about 2 cloves garlic
  a stick of horseradish root
½ cup vinegar
½ cup honey
  a ball of dill

Fill with hot water and seal. These are the ones my kids will always bring up when I send them to get a jar.

Now my mother, Mrs. Lydia Roth, took my recipe and changed it like this:

Mix the water, honey, salt and vinegar to taste in a kettle. Have the rest of the ingredients packed in the jar. Heat the liquid and pour over the pickles in the jars. Seal and set the jars into a canner or deep pan of water. Heat until it starts to boil. Set off and leave the jars in the water until it's cool. Hers are really good, crisp and clear. It takes a little longer, but if you have the time try them, too.

I have used cistern water and well water and either one works fine.

POTATOES

TWO RAW-POTATO PANCAKES

No. 1 (best)

Grate scrubbed unpeeled potatoes on grater so they look like coconut. Add 1 blended raw egg per medium potato. Add chopped onion; mix well. Brown in hot oil on both sides. Sprinkle seasoning over them when done.

No. 2 (fast)

Put one raw egg in blender. Cut up a scrubbed, unpeeled, potato and drop into the blender piece by piece. When done blending, add chopped onion. Brown on both sides in oil. Season. Do not make these until you are ready to fry them because the raw potatoes darken. This is true any time you are working with raw potato. Grate or blend only enough for one panful at a time.

USING COOKED POTATOES

As a rule potatoes are cheap. They are good and good for you. Cook enough and have a "potato meal," from the salad dressing to the dessert. Scrub your potatoes clean. Do not peel. Why persist in peeling foods and serving washed-out food at the table? The only time peeling potatoes is justified is if they are sprouting or really look tough. They can be peeled a whole lot faster for mashing after they are cooked. Wear rubber gloves for this purpose and you can handle the hottest potatoes with ease. What's the difference peeling them before or after? The difference is that what God put in them is still there when you eat them. For our own use we often scrub them and cut them up into pieces. We then mash them with the peelings on and in their own juice that they were cooked in. Add a little butter on the top. After eating them like this for a while you think they should always be that way. Another thing, do not drown them for cooking. They should *never* be cooked in so much water that the water has to be poured off. In a stainless steel waterless or copper bottom kettle use enough water to cover the bottom only. Start on high and switch to low immediately when it starts cooking. You will get so used to doing this that it becomes automatic with all vegetables. Save all water that any vegetables were cooked in and find a place where you can mix it in for a liquid. Never remove the lid during cooking or let steam escape.

SALAD DRESSING

¼ cup oil
¼ cup vinegar
¼ cup honey
1 egg

Add cooked potato pieces until thick. Add seasoning and chopped vegetable pieces: tiny pieces of celery, parsley, onion, pepper, herbs, seeds, dill. Make it up with what you like and what you have. Serve on your favorite greens, over fish, or cooked vegetables.

PLAIN POTATO PANCAKES

Add one beaten egg to approximately 1 cup or more of cooked mashed potatoes—fresh or leftover. Add chopped onion. Stir until smooth and brown in hot oil in frying pan. Season when done.

COOKED POTATOES

After the potatoes are cooked soft in their skins, peel them hot. Put one or two in the blender and add some of the hot cooking liquid. Blend this and you have something completely different to work with.

PASTE

First put some away for paste for the kids. It's cheap and it really sticks. Keep it in the refrigerator.

POTATO SOUP

Blend the potatoes until smooth in the blender with some of the cooking water. Blend the amount you want. For a smoother blend do not overload the blender; use about a cupful at a time. Pour into a saucepan. Now put in the blender any vegetables you have on hand—celery, parsley, carrots, green pepper and so on. Add enough water to blend these smooth and very fine. Mix into the hot potato mixture. Add some browned hamburger, seasoning, and you have a delicious soup with the vegetables still raw. But cooked vegetables can be used too and blended in, or they can be cooked right with the potatoes and blended all at once. Add your favorite spices or onions. Onions are very good with potato soup. The onions can be browned in with the hamburger.

PROTEIN PILLOWS

These can be a meal in themselves. Blend cooked potatoes to equal 1 cup. Put into bowl. Add 1 egg and stir in well.

Mix in soybean flour until dough hangs together fairly well—about ⅓ cup.

To form pillows, drop from tablespoon sideways into hot oil in pan. Brown on both sides. If you like onion, they are even better with chopped onion added. Sprinkle seasoning over them when done.

WHEAT GERM PILLOWS

Follow same directions using wheat germ instead of soybean flour.

CORN MEAL PILLOWS

Follow the same directions, except use corn meal for the flour.

ALL IN ONE

Try mixing all the flours above. For all these recipes, stir in just enough flour so that the mixture is stiff but still will drop easily from the spoon. Stir hard as that will make it thicker, too.

VEGETABLE PILLOWS

Add pieces of celery, green pepper, carrot, parsley, or whatever you have, to the liquid before you add the potatoes and the flour.

COOKED POTATO PUDDINGS

CAROB PUDDING

   3 eggs cooked in 1 cup water or
   3 hard boiled eggs
   1 cup hot water
Blend and add while running:
   4 tablespoons carob
   ½ cup honey
   1 teaspoon vanilla
Now while blender is running add cooked potato until thick, helping along on the top with the rubber scraper. Push the potato pieces down so the blade can catch them. It doesn't take much potato and they can be cold or hot. It doesn't matter because the mixture is hot from cooking the eggs or adding the hot water.

BANANA PUDDING

Same recipe as above only add one banana to the blender mixture and lemon or vanilla flavoring. Omit the carob. Pour over 2 or 3 sliced bananas. Serve soon because this darkens.

LEMON PUDDING OR SAUCE

Same recipe again, only add the juice of three lemons instead of banana or carob. Good with coconut added.

Vary or doll up any of these with different things. Pour them into a crust, add nuts, coconut, crumbs, marshmellos or whatever you can concoct.

If you have cooked potatoes on hand, there's an instant food waiting in your blender!

The customer says to the pretty waitress, "What's the fly doing in my soup?"

The waitress says, "I can't tell for sure but it looks to me like the back stroke."

INSTANT COOKED EGG PUDDINGS AND PIES

These are truly instant. They are thick immediately. You have your choice of using hard cooked eggs, or put ½ cup of water in a saucepan and bring it to a boil. Break three eggs into the boiling water and stir until they thicken. Omit this amount of water from the recipe. Put into blender and proceed with recipe. To use eggs in the shell, cut in half and scoop out the inside with a teaspoon. A desirable advantage with these puddings is that the fruits and the oils are added raw and stay raw. They are very tasty.

VANILLA PUDDING

3 cooked eggs
½ cup oil
¼ cup honey
½ cup water
1 teaspoon vanilla
¼ teaspoon almond

Blend together in blender.

Variation: Cinnamon or other spices, prunes, apples.

DATE PUDDING

1 cup water
3 cooked eggs
½ cup oil
1 cup cut up dates

Blend well. This is sweet, so do not add honey. For a stiffer pie add 1 tablespoon gelatin to the water first and blend until melted in. Flavor is like butterscotch. A few cut up dates and nuts can be added to the pudding.

FIG PUDDING

3 cooked eggs
1 cup water
1 cup figs
½ cup oil
1 heaped tablespoon honey

This gets very thick. Help along on top with rubber spatula. 1 cup of figs is about one-half of a 12-ounce package. Cut off the hard stem ends.

BANANA PUDDING
(A Sweet No Sweets)

3 cooked eggs
1 cup water
½ cup oil
3 bananas

Stir in 1 cut up banana in bowl or on top of pie. This is thick enough for pie, and sweet enough without honey.

CAROB PUDDING

      3 cooked eggs
      ¼ cup honey
      ½ cup oil
      1 cup water
    2½ tablespoons carob
          (add while blender is running)
      1 teaspoon pure vanilla

For pie, decrease water by ¼ cup or blend 1 tablespoon gelatin into the water first.

RAISIN PUDDING

      3 eggs
      ½ cup oil
      1 cup raisins
      ¾ cup water

Add ¼ cup whole raisins to bowl. This is thick enough for pie and naturally sweet.

The fruit sweetens some of these so that further sweetening is not necessary. Use these recipes as a basis and vary them with anything you have available. They thicken without any flour or starches. Use these as fillings for cake layers, especially the raisin, fruit or carob.

GELATIN PUDDINGS

BANANA PUDDING PIE

In blender:
      1 cup hot water
      1 heaping tablespoon gelatin powder

Let blender run for some time until gelatin is well melted. Add:

> 1 egg
> ¼ cup oil
> dash of vanilla

Add three cut up bananas while it is blending. Slice one banana in bottom of pie plate. Pour blender mixture over slices. Slice another banana over the top. Chill.

SOUR CHERRY PUDDING

In blender:

> 1 cup water
> 3 tablespoons plain gelatin

Blend until gelatin looks like whipped cream. Then, while blender is still running, add:

> 1 egg
> ½ cup honey
> 1 teaspoon pure vanilla
> ½ teaspoon pure almond
> ½ cup oil

Pour mixture into a bowl and set aside. Put in blender:

> 1 cup water
> 1 cup sour cherries (fresh or frozen)

Chop and blend until pink. Add to bowl mixture. Add one cup pitted sour cherries (whole) to bowl mixture.

Pour in baking pan and chill in refrigerator. Cut into bars.

Almond is compatible with cherry in any cherry dish.

PUMPKIN

PREPARE THE EASY WAY

Maybe it's laziness or lack of time that prompts a girl
—well—a woman to cut corners like this. This is a little
far out but it works. Wash a pumpkin, and release your
hostilities for the day by stabbing it a good one. Put it
on a pan and bake with or without water in the pan.
Now when the flesh is baked soft—you don't have to
wait until it caves in, it's soft before that—cut the
pumpkin in pieces and throw in the blender—peeling,
seeds and all. Strain and prepare your favorite way. I
usually throw the eggs and all in right away. It makes it
thinner for straining.

If you'd rather, you can scrape out the flesh with a
spoon and blend only that. It gets as smooth as any
commercial product. Put a cupful of pumpkin in the
blender. Then add eggs, spices, etc., from your favorite
recipe. The recipe for one pie usually fills the blender.
This pumpkin pie mixture is a good dessert baked without a crust—with or without nuts sprinkled on top.

Bake a few pumpkins at a time. Buy a basket full of
eggs and make up a large batch of pie mix. Freeze in
quart containers. Just put the frozen bulk in a baking
dish and bake. It will spread as it's baking. This is quick
and easy to fix.

USING RAW PUMPKIN

Anyone who is familiar with reading health magazines knows that raw pumpkin seeds are especially recommended for men and boys to eat because of a factor

in them which prevents or helps prostate troubles. Raw pumpkin seeds are available, but a cheap unexpected source is in every pumpkin that you cook up for pies. Just throw the pumpkin cut up in small cubes into the blender—peeling, seeds, and all. These are recipes for baked or raw pumpkin pudding or pie.

Peeling the skin first is up to you. It blends very well but try it both ways and decide for yourself whether to peel or not to peel. A small pumpkin makes three batches, or three blenders full. Blend long enough to make it good and smooth. Cuts the work of making pumpkin pie almost to nothing.

BAKED PUMPKIN PIE OR PUDDINGS

Follow recipe on pumpkin spice can.

In blender: 3 eggs and liquid called for in your recipe. Add molasses, spices, sugar (dark raw), or honey (full ½ cup). Turn blender on, take cover off and add pumpkin cubes and seeds until it gets thick. Bake in crust or alone for pumpkin pudding. Nuts can be sprinkled on the top.

RAW PUMPKIN PUDDING

- ¾ cup water (1 teaspoon gelatin for stiffer pie and use warm water)
- 2 to 3 tablespoons molasses
- 1 cup oil
- 2 or more tablespoons pumpkin pie spice (or to taste)
- ½ cup plus full tablespoon honey

Blend ingredients, and add raw pumpkin cubes and seeds until thick but still turning. Now cut 3 cooked eggs in half and scoop out the inside. Add to blender and blend well, until smooth.

Pour into dish and chill. Or, pour on crumb crust and

cover with more crumbs and sprinkle with cinnamon. Chill. For a stiffer pie add a tablespoon of gelatin to beginning of recipe in blender, and use warm water.

PUNCHES AND DRINKS

Punches and drinks don't need recipes. They only need the ingredients to mix and stir.

Use your blender throughout the year to prepare and store away juices and purees for punches (see Purees). It seems any juice lends itself to be mixed with other juices.

SOME IDEAS

Peppermint: Add hot water to a handful of leaves, blend and strain. Add honey and lemon for a fresh drink. Freeze in ice cubes or containers for winter use.

Rhubarb: Fill blender with rhubarb. Turn on and off to chop, then blend to mush. Strain. Very good drink fresh with honey and ice. Freeze some for winter or add honey right to the blender and make a puree. Blend raw frozen rhubarb all winter and strain for juice. Gives good flavor mixed with other juice.

All fruit purees that you have made from tame and wild fruits.

Fresh available fruit, lemons, oranges, grapes.

Grapes and small fruit like cherries can be blended, seeds and all, then strained through wire strainer.

Bottled raw juices.

Frozen orange and grape juices.

BROWN RICE

All rice mentioned in this book means brown rice. It's just the best for quality, flavor and nutrition. Cook a large batch of rice. For every cup of rice that you cook, bring to a boil 3 cups of water before you add the rice. Turn the heat to low and cover it tightly. When the rice has absorbed all the water it will be white, light and fluffy. You can always eat it plain or as a side course with your dinners. But all the secrets it can unlock in the blender!

OLD FASHIONED BAKED RICE
(dairyless)

Make 1 batch Magic Mix. Add it to 3 cups cooked rice, and thin with 3 cups water. Pour in large pyrex cake pan. Sprinkle 1 cup of raisins into the batter. Cover the top with cinnamon. Bake until center is set.

RICE BASE

    3   cooked eggs
    1   cup water or cook the 3 eggs in the cup of water
    1   cup oil

Blend until smooth. Add cooked rice until thick. Help turn on top with rubber scraper. This looks like a milk product, smells like it, and makes up like a milk product.

For using instead of sour cream: add a few drops of vinegar to base.

RICE MAYONNAISE

Take one cup of rice base and add honey, vinegar, and seasoning salt to taste. Make it as thick as you want it by adding more rice while you are blending. Good salad dressing or vegetable dip.

CHIP DIP

Use rice base plain or Rice Mayonnaise and add instant soup mix, and tiny pieces of onion, chives, parsley, chopped celery, celery seeds, fresh dill, dill seeds, etc. It is very similar to the dairy chip dips. Instant soup is available in health catalogues, too.

VANILLA TOPPING

For a dairy-like topping, use rice base above and add honey and vanilla. Or, add vanilla and a drop or two of almond. This is always smooth and will not harden in the refrigerator.

INSTANT PUDDINGS

1 cup cooked rice
1 cup water
3 cooked eggs, or cook the 3 eggs in the cup of water
½ cup oil
vanilla and almond or vanilla alone

For different flavors look under Cooked Egg Puddings, but use this recipe. Add in the order given and blend smooth.

LEMON SAUCE

Follow directions for pudding, except add the juice of about 3 lemons. Thicken with rice or leave thinner for a lemon sauce on cakes, etc. Omit the other flavorings.

RICE MAGIC MILK

Find at the beginning of the book.

RICE CARROT SALAD

Wash 3 or 4 carrots and cut into pieces. Put 1 cup warm water and 2 tablespoons gelatin in blender. Blend until gelatin is melted in. Add the juice of 2 lemons. Add 10 bioflavanoid tablets (optional) and blend. Add 1 cup cooked rice and blend until smooth. Throw in the carrot pieces and turn on and off only until they are chopped. Pour into bowl. Add 1 can of crushed pineapple or home canned. (1 pound can). Chill to set.

FRUIT SALAD

Same as Heavenly Rice with fruits of your choice.

HEAVENLY RICE

Make rice base. Add honey, vanilla and almond. Add a cup of whole cooked rice, Marshmellos, drained pineapple, nuts, banana slices just before eating. (Find the Marshmellos under Confections).

BROWN RICE SALAD

This rice salad makes its own dressing! Blend ½ cup honey, ½ cup oil, 1 teaspoon vanilla, 1 cup cooked rice, until smooth. Pour over 3 cups cooked rice and mix. Serve plain or dress up with fruit, cinnamon, pineapple, or dates.

TOMATOES AND TOMATO SAUCE DISHES

TOMATOES

There was a time when canning tomatoes started with a neat clean kitchen and ended with a watery mess everywhere. At least for me it did. Now I got smart in time—no more scalding or juice making—all thanks to my blender.

Gather the tomatoes: wash and pick out the ripest, choicest ones. These peel easily without scalding. Drop whole into jars and press down until jar is full. Process these for your salads and desserts.

Take the culls and cut off bad spots, and cut up with peelings and all. Drop in jars and process. Now for the blender. Empty a jar of culled tomatoes in your blender. Blend until smooth. Use this juice for salad dressings, soups, meat loaf, meat balls, or wherever you use tomato juice. For a thicker puree, drain the liquid and blend only the tomatoes. The peeling is blended very fine, but if you wish, it can be strained out along with the seeds through a wire strainer after blending.

I can put more fresh tomatoes down my kids in summer, when tomatoes are numerous, by blending them. Add a little honey, an ice cube or two (optional) and let them eat this with a spoon. This makes up many an afternoon snack and really is filling. Home-canned, culled tomatoes blended and strained are our winter juice.

Can your tomatoes this way and keep your kitchen cool; the only clean-up you have will be your sink.

SPANISH RICE

2 cups canned or raw tomatoes
1 tablespoon vinegar
1 tablespoon honey
½ cup cut up celery and celery leaves
½ cup onion, green pepper, and parsley pieces
1 teaspoon vegetable seasoning
   pimento pieces for color

Blend together only long enough to chop the vegetables fine. If the tomatoes are raw, blend them first alone. Pour over steamed brown rice and simmer awhile.

BAKED BEANS

Cook 1 pound dry beans until soft. Do not soak them. After they are cooked soft, prepare the sauce for them in the blender.

2 cups canned or raw tomatoes
1 tablespoon vinegar
1 teaspoon vegetable seasoning
⅓ cup honey
½ cup cut up celery pieces and leaves
¼ cup molasses
½ cup onion, green pepper, parsley pieces

Bacon pieces or bacon strips laid over the top of the beans.

Blend together only enough to blend the vegetables. If the tomatoes are raw blend them smooth first before adding the rest of the ingredients. The tomatoes can be strained but it's not necessary. Bake on low heat, 300°, until done.

To use up a surplus of tomatoes after frost or during the summer, can either of the above. Cook the beans and the rice first, then pour the sauce over them. Fill your jars and process the time required. For making a big batch of sauce blend several blenders of tomatoes. Then blend the other ingredients with a little tomato sauce. Mix in large container and add until taste is right. Once you know the taste you want, measurements are not necessary. From what I've read, people with sensitive stomachs can eat beans when they are blended. It's the pieces that cause the trouble. They aren't there when they are blended smooth.

USING CANNED TOMATOES

To strain or not to strain! Canned tomatoes, and raw, can be blended and strained or not. Strain them through a medium large wire strainer. This removes the seeds and the tiny peeling pieces. For drinking most people would prefer the juice strained. I like it with the seeds in. They taste good and are chewy. Also for a salad dressing the little red peeling pieces and the seeds, together with some little green things cut into it, such as parsley, green and red sweet pepper, celery, chives, dill, is very attractive. These are basic recipes, and to tell you the truth I never measure when I make a salad dressing or a meat sauce. I get a jar of tomatoes, see what's in the refrigerator, or run to the garden and get a few leaves and stalks of this or that. Empty the tomatoes into the blender and start adding. Start first with vinegar and honey, then the vegetable pieces or leaves, oil and last, seasoning. Now if you want more of this or that flavor, add more.

TOMATO GARLIC DRESSING
(this is the best)

Strain 1 quart canned tomatoes through wire strainer to remove juice. Blend the tomatoes and strain again to remove seeds.
In blender:
      the strained tomato puree
    1 clove garlic
    2 tablespoons honey
    ⅔ cup oil

Add vegetable seasoning to taste. Pour in jar and add 1 heaping teaspoon celery seed. If you make this ahead of time, the garlic clove can be dropped in to flavor the dressing. This one got many compliments.

TOMATO SAUCE FOR MEATS

    1 quart tomatoes (drained)
    ¼ cup vinegar
    ½ cup honey
    1 teaspoon salt seasoning

Pour over meat balls, roast, meat loaf, ribs, etc. The best way is to brown the meat first with chopped onions. Pour the tomato sauce over and finish cooking or roasting. The combination of browned meat, onions and this tomato sauce is good. To make it better add chopped vegetables, such as pepper, celery and celery leaves, parsley or spices. Onion or onion tops are better chopped and added with the meat, then blended into the sauce. For a variation try spiced vinegar, which you will find at the end of this chapter.

PLAIN SALAD DRESSING

Same as tomato sauce for meats, only add ½ cup of oil. Thick and creamy.

BLENDER CATSUP

    1 quart drained tomatoes
    ¾ cup each Spice Vinegar (at end of chapter), and honey
    1 teaspoon seasoning salt
    ½ teaspoon celery seed

Onion salt to taste or a little raw onion blended in. Have blender running and drop in tasting, a little at a time, until it's the way you want it. Onion can be omitted. Refrigerate.

PRETTY TOMATO DRESSING

1 cup canned tomatoes unstrained
1 cup raw celery, green pepper, and parsley pieces
1 tablespoon honey
¼ cup vinegar
½ cup oil
   seasoning salt

Turn blender on and off to mix and only enough to chop up the vegetables fine. Looks good on lettuce.

Raw tomatoes can be used in any of these tomato recipes. Blend the required amount smooth before adding the other ingredients. They also can be strained first to remove the peeling and seeds, but it isn't necessary.

When using canned tomatoes, make a quart do double duty. Use part of it for a meat sauce and take away a cupful to make a salad dressing. Again it's not necessary to depend entirely on a recipe. Use what you have and what you like and taste until it's the way you want. Always add less when you do this because more can always be added, but can't be removed if you get in too much.

COOKING KIDNEY

First cook kidney in water to remove bad taste and smell. Some kidneys are worse than others. When cooked, slice and put in pan. Cover with blender catsup, chopped onion, or tomato sauce with green vegetable pieces added. Simmer on low heat. Kan this be kidney?

TAVERNS

Brown two pounds of hamburger with a cup of chopped onion, in pan.

1 quart raw or canned tomatoes
¼ to ½ cup vinegar
½ cup honey
   seasoning to taste
1 cup celery or celery leaves

Blend fine, pour over browned meat and simmer. The longer it simmers on low heat, the better it gets. This can be made by pouring over raw hamburger too. Makes good hot sandwiches, or good on steamed rice or mashed potatoes.

MEAT BALLS OR MEAT LOAF DELUXE

First form meat balls out of solid hamburger, or ½ cup cooked rice, or ½ cup of rolled oats added to a pound of hamburger. The hamburger is already dead, so don't kill it again. Be gentle with hamburger and leave it loose—just so it barely hangs together. This makes the meat hold the juice and makes a light, juicy meat instead of a dry, packed one. Sprinkle ½ cup of chopped onion over a pound of meat.

To make meat loaf, form it into a loaf. Make it solid meat or add 1 egg, ½ cup of cooked rice, or ½ cup rolled oatmeal and ½ cup of chopped onion to a pound of meat. The onions can be sprinkled over the meat loaf too.

MEAT BALLS AND RICE

Cook brown rice 3 to 1. (3 cups of water to 1 rice.) When the rice has absorbed all the water, put in a large serving bowl. Build up a lake bed in the middle. Pour this lake bed full of meat balls and the sauce when they are done. Good for picnics.

DELUXE SAUCE FOR MEATS

½ clove garlic
2 cups canned tomatoes
¼ cup vinegar
3 tablespoons honey
1 cup mixed green vegetables: celery, pepper, parsley—mostly celery or celery leaves
  seasoning salt to taste
2 tablespoons cornstarch

Blend and pour over either raw meat balls or meat loaf. Or better yet, brown them first in the oven. Bake until done.

SALADS AND SALAD DRESSINGS

Let's start with basic mayonnaise. This is good in spring to dip all the radishes and salad leaves in right at the table. You can vary it with less vinegar, but remember that when it gets mixed with something the vinegar flavor diminishes. Also vinegars differ in acidity. From this basic recipe so many variations are possible. Here are a few. You might add:

Chopped pickle
Chopped relishes
Parsley
Celery stalk or leaf pieces, or seeds
Fresh dill or dill seed
Different flavored seasonings
Chives or onions
Garlic
Green or red sweet pepper
Cottage cheese
Herbs

BASIC MAYONNAISE

1 egg or 2 egg yolks
½ cup vinegar
½ cup honey
2 teaspoons vegetable seasoning

Blend and remove cover. While running, pour oil in the middle until it thickens and oil is lying on the top. You can turn it on and off to get the top oil in. Let it bubble up after stopping, and turn on again.

COOKED EGG MAYONNAISE

Same as above only use 2 whole cooked eggs or 3 cooked egg yolks.

The yolks do the thickening, so the whites can be used for something else. Now I have had trouble with some bottles of oil not thickening. The brand does not make any difference. I have used our own eggs out of the same basket and a salad dressing would not thicken. Then I've taken a new bottle of oil of the same brand, and still the same eggs, and that one would thicken. If you have such a bottle of oil, don't try it for another dressing, because that bottle will never thicken. If this should happen to you, it can still be used as a salad dressing. The flavor will be the same, only the texture will be different.

TARTAR SAUCE

Add chopped pickle, sweet and dill, chopped onion, and chopped parsley to Basic Mayonnaise. Good on fish.

PLAIN OIL DRESSING

Use one part each of honey and vinegar to two parts oil. Blend together and add flavor such as a piece of garlic, onion, etc.

117

PLAINER YET

One part vinegar to 2 parts oil. Add your favorites either to the salad or the dressing. If you rub the salad bowl with garlic, you won't need any in the dressing. If you add onion or onion greens to the salad you don't want them in the dressing. Seasoning can also be sprinkled right on the salad when you're tossing it.

SEED DRESSINGS

Any dressing can be made with sesame or sunflower seeds, using the seeds for the oil. Blend until thick and smooth.

CABBAGE SAUERKRAUT

Fill blender with cabbage, turn on and off until chopped. Keep pushing it down until it all gets blended to a mush.

Slice more cabbage very thinly with knife on cutting board. Add a little salt and mix with the mush in a bowl. Pack tightly into sterilized jars. Push down hard so juice comes up and covers cabbage. Seal and let cure a few weeks. Hint: Sterilize the jars easily. Put in oven and set temperature at 300° for about a ½ hour.

COLE SLAW
(Waterless Method)

½ cup honey
½ cup vinegar

Put in blender and fill blender with cabbage pieces. Turn blender on and off to chop cabbage and help by pushing the large pieces of cabbage down. When chopped drain through large wire strainer and use the juice for the next blender full. Repeat as often for as much as you need. The juice can be left in the last batch. Season as wanted. Do not let the blender run when chopping vegetables. Only turn it on and off letting it come to a complete stop in between. Garnish with mustard or celery seed. Garnishes are found at end of this salad chapter.

EASY CABBAGE SLAW

Add cabbage pieces to blender, half filled with cold water. Blend on low until cabbage has all been pulled in. Strain through wire strainer and repeat using same water again if you are making a larger batch. If you don't have a low speed on your blender, turn it on and off until cabbage is all shredded. The longer it chops the finer it gets.

To add carrots, peppers, celery or other vegetables, it is better to chop and strain each separately. Because they are all different textures, they tend to chop differently.

Finish the cole slaw with Basic Mayonnaise. To make it really good and extra special add garnishing such as celery seeds. A small onion added gives real good flavor and can be added to the water to flavor all the slaw. Add small pieces of pimento and parsley pieces for color.

NOW, don't throw away this vitamin rich water when you have finished making the salad. Add a little papaya or some other juice and make a drink. Or you can work it into soup, gravy, and even the punch! (without onion for the punch, please.)

SWEET SALAD DRESSING

This dressing will keep indefinitely in the refrigerator. It is very convenient to have on hard at all times. After you add it to your salad give the salad a few brisk stirs. This fluffs up the dressing so it gets white and no one can tell that it's not whipped cream.

1 egg
½ cup honey
1 teaspoon vanilla
¼ teaspoon almond flavoring

Start blender with everything in and take off the cover. Add oil while it is running until it's thick and lying on top. Once you have it this way the longer it runs the thicker it gets. Use for any fruit or sweet salad where otherwise you might use cream.

CABBAGE DELIGHT SALADS

1. Slice cabbage and toss with Sweet Salad Dressing.
2. Slice cabbage and add sliced bananas. Toss with sweet dressing. Bananas and cabbage are a good flavor combination.
3. Slice cabbage, banana, unpeeled apple, and toss with dressing.
4. Slice cabbage, banana, apple, and add raisins and nuts. Toss with sweet dressing. Give all these a brisk stir to fluff up the dressing.

BROWN RICE SALAD

Cook extra rice when you prepare rice. Keep the other cold for a salad. Toss cold rice with sweet salad dressing. Stir to fluff the dressing. To vary this add fruit —pineapple, cinnamon, raisins or chopped dates.

RELISHES

If you have a way of keeping your carrots, beets, etc. in a cellar or cave, or have access to fresh vegetables all winter, why put up any relishes at all? The raw relishes are so good and don't have the life cooked out of them. Make any raw relish taste like a canned relish like this.

Take some of your dill or sweet pickles. In the blender either mix ½ cup of honey and vinegar, or use your pickle juice, or some of both. Make it to taste before you start. Now drop in pieces of raw carrots, beets, cauliflower, celery or any other raw vegetable; or use frozen raw corn, cabbage, peppers, etc. Turn the blender on and off never leaving it run, until they are chopped. Add pickle pieces last because they are the softest. Such a colorful relish you never could can, and keep the colors. Drain the relish through a wire strainer and use the liquid over for as many batches as you make. Chop the beets separately as their juice would make the whole relish pink.

EXTRA SPECIAL
RAW BEET RELISH

Put ½ cup each honey and vinegar in the blender. Chop amount of beets wanted. Drain through a wire strainer and use the juice over as often as necessary. Save the juice and make Pretty Pink Dressing (next recipe). This gives beets a really delightful flavor.

PRETTY PINK DRESSING

Always save the liquid from the relishes that you make raw. They have some of the nutrients soaked away in them that were in the beets or other vegetables. In blender:

> the strained red juice (should make a cupful; if it doesn't, add equal amounts of honey and vinegar to make a cupful)
>
> 1 whole egg or 2 egg yolks
> 1 scant tablespoon vegetable seasoning

Turn on medium to high speed on your blender and add oil until it thickens. These beet recipes make quite a hit when I'm demonstrating blenders. I suppose it's because the beet is a hard vegetable to please tastes with. There will always be some people who just won't touch beets, but a lot have changed their minds having tasted these.

RAW CARROT RELISH

Make the same as beet relish.

PRETTY GOLDEN ORANGE DRESSING

Use the juice from making the carrot relish in place of the honey and vinegar in the Basic Dressing recipes.

BRIGHT GREEN AVOCADO DRESSING

1 egg
¼ honey
¼ vinegar
1 or 2 avocadoes

Use nice soft ripe avocado. This is the oil and will thicken very thick. For Christmas add red pimento.

RAW RADISH DIP

In blender:
½ cup vinegar
½ cup honey

Add radish pieces until blender is ½ full of radishes—turning on and off until radishes are shredded as fine as desired. Serve at once or refrigerate. Keeps well as a raw relish. Then air out the kitchen as this is akin to cooking cabbage.

CANNED RADISH RIP RELISH

This uses up the tough and large radishes, even if some are already in bloom. It is the prettiest pink relish due to the red in the radishes, either raw or canned. See how many people are able to identify what it is, after you have it canned!

Set three pints or four ½ pints in oven—turn on to 300°.

In saucepan:

    1 cup vinegar
    1 cup honey
    2 tablespoons pickling spices

Heat and simmer to release flavors of spices. Watch carefully, as it foams up if heat is too high. Use a large enough kettle to avoid its foaming over. While this is simmering cut up radishes into fourths or pieces and fill blender with cut up radishes.

Strain the hot spicy mixture through a wire strainer into the blender. Turn on and off and shred until all radishes are pulled down and cut up. Put back into saucepan and add 1 tablespoon mustard seed. Heat until foamy and bubbly. Take hot jars out of oven and spoon hot relish into each, in turn, to avoid cracking jars. Rinse lids with hot water and seal. This is a delicious disguise of an unexpected vegetable!

COLD POTATO SALAD

Cook potatoes in their jackets. Peel and dice. Mix with any of the mayonnaises in this book. For added flavor add diced onion, pimento and chopped pickle or relish. Hard cooked eggs can be sliced or diced in.

DEVILED EGGS
(speed method)

Cut hard boiled eggs in half, and scoop out the insides with a teaspoon. Put the yolks in the blender and make like Cooked Egg Mayonnaise only using all the yolks you have.

Or to make them as usual, peel hard boiled eggs, cut the long way in half, and mix the yolks with mayonnaise. Here again little pieces of chopped greens or pimento pepper are good. Sprinkle with paprika. To send along with lunch boxes, cut in half around the middle, scoop out, put the white in a nut cup and fill in the yolk filling.

SALAD SANDWICH FILLINGS
(speed method)

To prepare eggs in a hurry for a tuna salad or ham salad, etc., just scramble them in a little butter or boiling water and add to the meat. Toss with mayonnaise. Add variations.

HOT GERMAN POTATO SALAD

This is so good hot or cold that my family would rather have this for lunch than anything else. It's also good for lunch boxes.

Wash potatoes with skins on. Cut into cubes to make close to a gallon of cut up cubes.

Slice three large onions or about the same amount of new onions and green tops.

In blender:

    1½ cups vinegar
    ¾ cup honey
    1 cup oil
    2 teaspoons vegetable seasoning

Blend until creamy and pour over cut up potatoes and onions. Cover tightly. Start on high heat; and turn down to low; cook until done. Stir briskly so the starch from the potatoes thickens the juice. The bigger the potatoes the more starch and the thicker the juice.

Serve hot. Keep the rest in the refrigerator to eat cold. It's good either way.

For plain left over cold potatoes, mix up the above dressing and pour over. Heat. By cooking the potatoes in the dressing all the valuable minerals are kept intact.

SPICE VINEGAR

    1 cup vinegar
    1 cup honey
    ⅓ cup mixed pickling spice

Make a large batch and keep some on hand in the refrigerator for making raw relishes, dressings, or wherever you would like to use it.

Large Batch

3 cups vinegar
3 cups honey
1 box of pickling spice

A word of caution: Watch the red peppers in the pickling spice. If you don't want it too peppery, watch how many fall in and keep some back. If you like it peppery, leave it as is. Some boxes have more in than others.

MUSTARD SEED GARNISHING

Cook 1 box mustard seed in 1 cup vinegar and 1 cup of honey. Simmer until mustard seeds are soft and swelled up. Add a tablespoon to salads, relishes, or whatever they would garnish. Good in cole slaw or other cabbage dishes. Add after salad is mixed. Don't blend them in.

MUSTARD

For making your own mustard for meats, blend the whole business smooth.

HORSERADISH

Dig up and wash horseradish roots.

Mix equal amounts of honey and vinegar and throw horseradish into the blender. Turn on and off or whatever you have to do to get it blended. If you don't own a gas mask, you'll just have to suffer through it like I do.

Now that it's blended you can eat it in this fire stage or mix it with any of the salad dressings in this book. A little added to a salad dressing is real tasty. Add it to the extent of your love for horseradish.

Horseradish keeps a long time in the refrigerator.

SALAD TIPS

We have a large garden, so we have most of our own vegetables. Our garden never sees any insecticides, so I can use all the leaves and tops with confidence! These are some of the ways of keeping over vegetables for winter use that I like.

Celery is good cut up, stalks, leaves and all, and frozen raw. Freeze it on a cookie sheet and put in containers. Pour out needed amount for adding to dressings, soups, etc.

Cabbage is also good cut up and frozen raw, as above. Use in salads.

Onion tops from hardy onions that come up every year and the little onions that form on the top, are good frozen raw. This almost eliminates planting onions as they are the first up in the spring and the last to freeze down in the fall. The name of these is Egyptian onions.

Cucumber can be frozen raw sliced. I'm not too fond of them though. Pack both onions and cucumbers in tight glass jars.

Peppers are good frozen raw.

Parsley is good frozen raw.

Rhubarb is good frozen raw.

In the spring instead of cutting lettuce, pull out the nicer plants, roots and all. This makes it easier to wash with all the leaves intact. Then stick roots in water as flowers in a vase. It will stay fresh so much longer as the root absorbs the water. The row will last just as long too, because this gives all the small plants a chance to mature as the row thins.

Onion scallions are as good flavored as the onions themselves.

TAPIOCA FLOUR

Tapioca flour can be purchased in the health stores. Tapioca can be ground up finer than it is in the blender but not as fine as what one can buy. It also gets quite hot when grinding it, as is the case with trying to grind any grain to flour. It is better to purchase these where they can be ground without heating. Tapioca flour is very handy as it thickens in just no time at all. Don't try to smooth out any lumps after it is cooked in the blender because it thins and will not thicken again.

VEGETABLES

Save the juice from canned or cooked vegetables for making purees for soups or for baby. Or use it in gravies or cooking.

Another way is to thicken the juice, heat the vegetables with half of the liquid, and put the other half in the blender. Add a pat of butter, 3 tablespoons cornstarch and seasoning. Pour into the hot vegetables and allow to thicken on low heat. This is for 1 quart of vegetables.

VEGETABLE PUREE

Most vegetables can be blended to a puree raw. Put the pieces into the blender and turn on and off to chop fine. Help push down with rubber scraper. When fine turn on and blend smooth. If it's a vegetable that won't juice to a puree, add some liquid from cooking vegetables. Celery and cabbage blend well to a puree and the juice can then be strained. Carrots are too dry and need something added to help.

PART II

BLENDERBUSZ

BLENDING WHOLE GRAINS

This chapter on using whole grains and your blender is not for farmers only. Whole cleaned grains can be bought from millers and places that specialize in flours and grains. Here in our area any whole cleaned grain can be purchased from the Sioux Miller in Sioux City, Iowa. If you make an effort, you too can hunt up a source for your kitchen. Most farmers will sell some and elevators that buy the grain from the farmer.

Whole grains and seeds that *still grow* have been found in tombs, caveman's caves and ancient excavations. This should be ample enough proof how well whole seeds keep their potency. But, once the seed is ground, the meal loses quality every day in storage, finally reaching the point of becoming rancid.

It takes no time at all worth mentioning to dry grind cereal grains in the blender. They are ground to cereal consistency before the water is boiling to cook them in. And that flavor! There's really something special and d'fferent about fresh ground cooked cereal!

Here is a list of the grains that I have worked with and what I've found out about them.

THE SOFT GRAINS

Wheat—tasty chewy and nut-like flavor.

Barley—hulled, chops and cooks to the consistency similar to tapioca or a larger cream of wheat. This hulled barley is what is used for soup cooking and found in canned soups. Very chewy, very good.

Rye—This does not taste anything at all like com-

131

mercial rye bread, but rather has a malted taste like the malt in malted milks, ranking high in good flavor.

Flax—Here's a surprise! It cooks thick and gooey. The flavor is similar to co-co wheat. Try it and see! Tastes like cocoa is added only it has this gooey consistency that is different.

Oats—hulled, has the same flavor as steel-cut oats or oatmeal, only a little better because of the freshness.

The soft grains, mostly wheat, are used by blender demonstrators to show the grinding power of the blender they are trying to sell. Some blenders do have a better grinding ability than others, but for grinding cereals they are all capable of doing the job.

THE HARD GRAINS

Corn—I think most people are familiar with the flavor of corn meal mush.

Brown Rice—This is my family's favorite. Use this one to get yours started on enjoying whole grain cereals, because you can tell them it's cream of wheat and get by with it. Later after they are used to it, show them that you are grinding brown rice.

Millet—This has a sharp flavor all its own, but cooked with a ½ or a cup of raisins and served with brown raw sugar, it's quite good.

Soybeans—Grind, turn into a hot frying pan and brown by stirring on medium heat until browned and smelling good. Cover with water and cover and simmer on low heat until soft. Add more water if needed. These browned ground soybeans taste just like the ones used by the bakeries on rolls that taste and look like ground peanuts. They soften fast when used as a crumb base or cereal or any place that has moisture for them to absorb.

If you have to cook for only one or two persons, whole grains are better to keep and store than any packaged food, because of the keeping qualities. Store them in glass and in a cool place, if possible, to keep out insects.

GRAIN VALUES

In a book entitled *Shall We Eat Bread* by R. W. Bernard (A.B., M.A. Ph.D.) and Enrenfried E. Pfeiffer, M.D., which Mr. L. J. Knauf of Milwaukee sent me, these authors place millet, rice, corn, wild rice, above rye, barley, oats, and last of all wheat. One of the reasons is that the first four grains mentioned are alkaline grains and the rest are acid forming grains. Aside from this are the allergy factors plus numerous other reasons that I won't go into. This book is available from Health Research, Mokelumne Hill, California.

COOKING CEREALS

Put specified amount of water in saucepan on high heat to start cooking while you are grinding the grain in the blender. All these recipes are to serve 6. The amount of whole grains given is *before* grinding. For best results grind only one cup or not more than 1½ cups of grain at a time in any blender.

Wheat—Stir 2 cups of ground wheat into 1 quart boiling water. Stir hard until it's smooth. Put on the cover and turn off the burner and let it set for a while. Stir hard to thicken before serving.

Barley—Grind 1½ cups hulled barley and stir into 1 quart of boiling water. Cover and let set to fully fluff the kernels. White and chewy.

Rye—2 cups rye ground to one quart of water. Same procedure.

Flax—2 cups flax ground, to one quart of water. Serve immediately.

Oats—1½ cups hulled oats, ground to one quart water. Cover awhile.

Millet—Grind 1½ cups millet, 1 cup raisins (whole) to 1 quart water.

Rice—1 cup of brown rice, ground to 1 quart of water. (Cream of Rice)

Soybeans—Method given under hard grains.

Corn—1½ cups whole corn to 4 cups water. Left-over corn cereal can be sliced cold and served as any corn meal mush.

If you have bought grains that have not been cleaned, you can wash the grain in a wire strainer under a faucet and grind it wet. I like dry grinding the best, though.

Whole Cooked Brown Rice—Cold or hot, also makes a good cereal eaten with milk, etc. as any cereal. (Add a touch of vanilla.)

Popped Popcorn—Whole or chopped in the blender is a good *puffed* cereal, with the taste similar to puffed rice, but still very chewy.

USING LEFTOVER COOKED CEREAL

There is a real advantage in cooking too much cereal, because it makes such good instant puddings. Also the ingredients in the pudding stay raw, the oil, the honey, the eggs. If you have purchased raw unheated pressed oils, any recipe that calls for the use of that oil to remain unheated will preserve the vitamin E content. These puddings have a cooked taste and texture without starches or cooking.

WHOLE GRAIN PUDDINGS
(dairyless)

I am going to give only one recipe, as all variations can be made on this one. Change it to suit your tastes and try different flavors. If you want to use milk, use it in place of water.

In blender:

    1 cup cooked cereal (any leftover cold cereal)
    ¼ cup water
    ¼ cup oil
    ¼ cup raw sugar or honey
    1 teaspoon vanilla
    2 egg yolks or 1 cooked egg

Start blender and help along, stirring on the top, as it gets pretty thick and is hard on the blender. Ready to serve.

CAROB CEREAL PUDDING

Add three tablespoons carob powder and help along on the top, because this gets thicker than the plain.

For an attractive pudding make a batch of plain and of carob and pour the carob into the plain giving a few stirs to give it a marbelized effect. Dried fruits, coconut, nuts, bananas, or you name it, anything should enhance these puddings. But, watch it so you don't add anything watery or it will get thinner.

FROZEN PUDDINGS

By the way, any of these puddings in this book can be frozen and eaten while icy, which is a way to feed children a whole grain cereal put up in pudding form. It's a rare child that doesn't go for something frozen.

SOYBEAN PUDDING

This requires 2 or 3 tablespoons more cooked soybean cereal to get it thick. Save some of the cooked roasted soybean cereal to add to the pudding. Gives the flavor of chopped roasted peanuts.

MERINGUES

Make these puddings seem special by making a meringue with the leftover egg whites and browning them on a buttered pan in mounds in a hot oven. Place one browned mound on each serving of the pudding. Meringues are very good sweetened with honey too. Beat the egg whites very stiff and beat in enough honey to taste (about 1 tablespoon to each egg white). Add vanilla and almond flavorings. I like to add a teaspoon of vanilla and ¼ teaspoon almond to a recipe when using honey. Unless carob is in a recipe, then vanilla alone is best. If you have time, let the meringues brown a little, then turn the oven off and leave them in to bake clear through. They can stay in until the oven is cool. They can be shaped with a depression and baked. Fill the depression with pudding. A novelty to get the kids to like it.

Pudding Color—Most of these puddings are a cream color when finished.

Malted Pudding—Use cold cooked rye cereal.

Flax Pudding—Good, but has a gooey texture.

MIXED CEREALS AND PUDDINGS

I have given each grain separately with the cooking instructions. But they can be mixed and ground together in any combination that you would want. The cost is less and whole grains stay fresher. If you buy a ground mixed cereal, it will cost you more and it loses quality every day in storage. We could all bring the cost of living down, especially where there is a larger family, by starting to use fresh natural foods such as whole grains. A side benefit could also be better teeth and health and fewer medical expenses.

Once you become used to making these cereals in the morning, you'll find that it really doesn't take much more time than setting out the cereal boxes. Keep any leftover cereal and make a pudding, if you can keep it that long. My kids will eat it cold during the day as cereal if they find it.

A fun thing that I like to show at a blender demon-

136

stration is to first grind the grain, usually rice, cook it quickly in an electric fry pan, then remove a cupful and put it in the blender. Add the ingredients given for the pudding, and then add a cold squashed fried egg.

Picture this in your mind: a blender jar with cooked wheat, or rice, oil, honey, water and a cold squashed fried egg in it! It looks pretty ickey! These could all be leftovers from breakfast. Then when the blender is turned on and it starts to thicken, I add 3 tablespoons of carob and help along on top to get it thick and smooth. Now the expressions change somewhat: It looks pretty good—but they still remember what all was thrown into it. So, I pass it around and let everyone taste it, and that's when the expressions change again—to surprise! Surprise that it tastes that good! Something like this is especially overwhelming to people who don't grind their own cereal or even know that it's possible to do so!

FRESH UNCOOKED CEREAL GRAINS

There are seeds that don't require cooking, only grinding. The blender does a good job on these and they are good and tasty. Serve the same way as any cereal, with milk and sugar or honey. They are good alone or in combination. They grind so fast and you have something really fresh and good tasting. These are the ones that we've tried and what we found out about them.

Sunflower Seeds—These cost from around 79c a pound and up. Sunflower seeds always taste good and so they also make a tasty cereal, easy to grind in any blender.

Pumpkin Seeds—are good alone, but not as mild

tasting as sunflower seeds are. You might like them better in combination with other seeds.

Flax—does not require cooking to get thick. It seems to thicken in anything after it is ground. Has a nut-like or bran-like flavor.

Sesame Seeds—are high in calcium. Good tasting. Add a little touch of vanilla along with the milk and sugar.

Mom's Mischief—Your offspring do not like what's good? Try vanilla! I've never found a kid yet that doesn't like vanilla. Add vanilla to the cereal or make a big deal of their adding it themselves. Vanilla blends well with these fresh ground seeds.

Do you know that the ingredients are listed on a packaged product in the order of their weight or volume? Most ready-to-eat cereals have sugar as the second highest ingredient. On some cereals you'll find it on the top. That means that they contain more sugar than anything else. By serving a freshly ground cereal, cooked or other, it contains no added sugar and you'll find you won't put any more on when you eat it than the packaged ones.

CEREAL CORDIAL
(mixed to your taste)

Blender chop any amount from the following list and mix to your taste.

Sunflower seeds
Pumpkin seeds
Sesame seeds
Flax seeds
Pecans, walnuts or any flavorful nut
Chia seeds, ground or whole
Dried apples, pears, apricots, peaches
Dark dried fruits such as pitted prunes or dark raisins
Ground dates (These date tidbits can be purchased
    ready to add.)

Now, if you wish you can add an equal amount of a bran dry cereal, purchased either in the grocery, or one of the delicious dry ready-to-eat cereals available in health stores. Mix it all up and you have something really good!

Also, you can roast a small part of the seeds, either in the oven or in a hot pan on the stove and chop them for adding. Gives another flavor to enhance this cereal. But, DO leave the greater part of it raw! The dried fruits should be chopped separately, preferably by hand.

Once you start developing a taste for this sort of thing, you might want to try ordering dried fruits, seeds, and nuts from some of the growers that advertise in magazines like *Natural Foods and Farming, Prevention,* or *Let's Live.* These are dried without preservatives and grown organically and once you taste these, the supermarket products seem dull. As far as cost goes, there is nothing cheap about any cereal, in fact per ounce it's high and for a family like mine a box of cereal isn't near enough for one meal. If you have another seed or nut that you like and it's not mentioned above, add what you like. Fresh diced fruit is good served along with this cereal, such as sliced bananas or strawberries.

FLAX BREAKFAST PUDDING

As I've said before, flax will thicken a liquid that it's put into after it is ground. This pudding can be a complete breakfast. Top it with some fresh fruit if you like and you'll have your eggs, cereal and fruit!
In blender:

139

2 egg yolks
½ cup of honey or raw sugar
¼ cup oil
1 cup whole cleaned flax
1 teaspoon vanilla

Turn on blender and gradually add
2 cups water

Add only enough water at a time to keep the mixture moving, so that the seeds blend as fine as possible. After the blender gets quite full, help along on the top because the mixture gets quite thick. Everything stays raw in this.

SOAKED FLAX

Whole flax soaked a few hours or overnight makes delicious eating, too. At our house Junie likes to soak flax and eat it. It doesn't need anything done to it except to cover with about an inch or so with water. It will soak up and thicken, and you can add more water if you wish. It also can stand until it's sprouting. This is a fun thing to chew on and would also be a good breakfast cereal, if you remember to soak some the night before. Stir it once in a while and add water if it needs it.

MAKING YOUR OWN GRANOLA

In blender or Mitey Mill:
Grind ¼ cup unsweetened coconut to make ½ cup after it's ground. (You can use sweetened, but the flavor won't be as good.)

In a fry pan (preferably cast iron), with the burner turned on HI, put:
¼ cup soybean oil
¼ teaspoon salt
⅓ cup turbinado sugar

Stir until grainy or lumpy-looking and add:
the ½ cup ground coconut
¼ cup sesame seeds

140

Keep stirring very briskly and when it starts to brown nicely, add:

2 cups regular rolled oats.

Keep stirring briskly until the oats start to brown. If you have an electric stove, you can turn it off and the heat from the burner and the pan will finish browning it just right. Otherwise, keep turning very briskly so none scorches and ruins the flavor. Turn out of the pan at once. Let cool a bit and add:

¼ cup raw sesame seeds

½ cup raw wheat germ

Have all the ingredients ready before you start because once the pan is hot and the browning starts, you dare not leave it or stop stirring! If you aren't sure of the color to brown it, have a package of the commercial brand beside you the first time. This will have more sesame in it than the commercial brand will, but that's the advantage of making your own. You can add more value. Being able to leave some of it raw is a definite advantage.

Don't try making a larger batch. This has to be made in smaller batches, like jelly, so it gets nicer. If you have never tried the commercial brand and aren't acquainted with this good flavor, you've missed something. Kids go for this stuff. The color when done is a medium brown with darker brown flecks and pieces in it. The oatmeal will not all darken; some of it will brown and some will stay lighter.

This is a new recipe added for this edition.

HONEY

Now with honey there can be quite a difference in flavors. Not only in the flavor of the flowers that it's made from, but in the locality that it comes from. We purchased honey from various areas and find that clover honey for example can have a different flavor and color than another area does. The clover honey from this midwest area seems to be the mildest in flavor of any honey that we have used. But don't take my word for it, because we haven't tried enough to be sure of this. Anyway, the same recipes can be changed in the flavor of the honey used.

Fallflower—stronger and darker, good in combination with carob in recipes.

Sugar—raw, white or brown—will give the same flavor everywhere it's used and can be substituted in any of these recipes using a little less or the same amount as honey.

Proverbs 24, verse 13—My son, eat thou honey because it is good; and the honey-comb which is sweet to thy taste.

EASY HONEYLIZED OR CARAMELIZED POPCORN

The first time I tasted this was at our neighbors, Allen Orths. She made popcorn with white sugar and called it sugar popcorn. We make it with either raw sugar or honey. It can be made ahead because it gets like cracker jack. This method of making honeylized popcorn I had published in *Prevention* magazine, January, 1967, and will repeat it here.

This requires an old style popcorn popper with a handle on the top for turning it. Put ⅛ cup each oil and honey and ½ cup popcorn in the popper. Turn the burner on HI and keep turning like mad to keep it from scorching. If it's an electric stove, turn it off after it starts popping. Turn it out into a bowl fast. This takes a little practice, and if you do burn a batch, wash the popper before using it again. Sprinkle the popcorn with cinnamon while it is hot if you like it. Once you are successful in making this, it is a real treat. Don't pop it too long as the time between popping and burning is short. It's better to leave a few unpopped kernels than to let them burn.

Making caramel corn with brown or raw sugar is not as touchy as with honey but the method is the same. To really make it good use either part oil and part butter or all butter and a dash of vanilla.

CARAMEL CRUNCH CANDY

In saucepan:
    1 cup honey
    1 cup sunflower seeds
Bring to a rolling boil on medium heat, then turn heat to lowest setting and let simmer until bubbles are brown and very thick and it coats the spoon heavy. Take off the stove and add:
    3 heaping tablespoons of carob powder
    1 teaspoon of vanilla
    1 cup of raw sunflower seeds
Stir in with good strong spoon and stir until mixture is a lump. If it isn't cooked long enough it will take more beating to thicken it. Turn into a buttered pyrex cake or pie pan and press in with a spatula that has been buttered to keep from sticking.

143

Peanuts—Use raw peanuts, but you have to cook all of them with the mixture because raw peanuts are almost impossible to eat.

Pumpkin Seeds—Do the same, cook half of them for a roasted flavor and add half of them raw. They are good using half pumpkin and half sunflower seeds in a candy.

Now, you can mix any seeds here, cooking half of them gives a delicious cooked flavor and adding half raw leaves some nutrition in the candy.

Carob powder can be omitted and they are more caramel-like, but beat the finished cooked dough a long time to get it stiff.

Unsweetened coconut cooked along with the honey and seeds is very good.

RAW EGG WHITES

I've read in health magazines and the Grolier Encyclopedia on science that raw eggs are healthier for you if you don't eat too many raw egg whites. That's why in most of these recipes you have a choice of using a whole egg or only the egg yolks. I like to save the egg whites and bake meringues for toppings. It makes any pudding or dessert attractive and appetizing. If you distrust your source of eggs and don't want to use them raw, substitute cooked eggs. Cooked eggs will make the mixture thicker and change the flavor somewhat.

WHOLE GRAINS IN BAKING

Pancakes and quick breads are also fast and easy to make from whole grains. As to the fineness in grinding, not all blenders grind the same. Some do grind finer than others. The soft grains grind quite near to flour, but the hard grains grind only so fine, usually leaving some larger particles. The secret here is not to over-bake. Remove the baked goods as soon as they are done but not any overdone. Any over-baking will dry and make the bigger particles hard. If you take it out just as it's done they will be soft. Yes, the grinding does make the flour heated, but you add the rest of the ingredients and bake the batter right away to preserve the freshness.

In using whole grains in baking use the same amount as the flour called for in a recipe as a substitution.

The whole grains that can be ground fresh in the blender and used to make quick breads are

Whole Wheat
Whole Rye
Hulled Oats
Whole Corn
Whole Millet

CORN

There is something really good about fresh ground corn used in recipes—good tasting and good for you. Not only that, but it's cheap too. A bushel of shelled corn can be bought for under $1.50 and you can bake up a storm with a bushel of shelled corn.

In the February, 1967, *Let's Live* magazine there is an article about the Aztec's corn diet and their energy. It states that there are still many Indians who live on corn and are stronger and healthier than the best fed Americans. This is a very good article and worth reading.

Most shelled corn is clean. About all that's necessary is to remove odd pieces of husk or cob as you pour it into the cup.

These recipes are the same as in Part I, but I'll repeat

them using whole corn. I've tried popcorn (unpopped) for these, but it's too hard. Regular corn is softer.

TORTILLAS

Put one cup of whole corn into the blender, grind dry, or with one cup of water. Let blend and grind for some time, then add three eggs one by one. Bake in hot pan or griddle with a dab of butter. Brown on both sides. Stir batter each time, to stir up what settles to the bottom. Makes about 8 tortillas. If you dry grind it fine first, add the cup of water next before the eggs.

CORN BREAD
(or other grains such as wheat, oats, rye, or millet)

Dry grind 1½ cups of corn, add gradually, while blender is running,

    1 cup of milk or water
    3 eggs one by one
    ½ cup of oil
    and last of all 1 tablespoon baking powder

Add these ingredients gradually and keep it blending. Bake in buttered pyrex cake pan at 400° only until set. Keeping the mixture thick while blending makes it finer too.

This recipe can be used for any quick bread recipe using any whole grains. Now here's another recipe using whole grains for making pancakes or griddle cakes.

PANCAKES
(using any whole grain on preceding list)

    1 cup whole kernels, grind fine dry or with
    1 cup of milk or water,

Then add:
    ½ cup oil
    3 eggs
    1 tablespoon baking powder
Bake on hot griddle or pan, using butter with the first one to prevent sticking.

For waffles: Separate the eggs, using the yolks in the blender and beating the whites very stiff. Add the baking powder to the egg whites and pour the blender mixture over, folding it in.

If you don't want to use baking powder, they get good without it by beating the egg whites stiff separately. This goes for breads and muffins too. Either one of these two recipes can be used for muffins. Using baking powder will make a lighter, higher product.

When baking pancakes, where you beat the egg whites separately, give the center plenty of time to bake through before turning them over. They need a longer baking time to set the center. Don't have the heat too high, because they will brown too fast and be raw on the inside.

Milk makes a better bodied product than water; but to convert recipes using milk to dairyless, use ¾ cup water and another egg in place of 1 cup milk.

Ruth of the Bible gleaned corn, barley and wheat in the fields of Boaz. How much would she have appreciated a blender to throw those grains in after the hard work of gleaning in the fields? Ruth—Chapter 2.

GRINDING FLOURS

The blender is not a flour mill. The longer it grinds the hotter the grain becomes. Therefore buy your flours at a mill that doesn't produce that much heat during grinding. It's all right to use it if you are in a pinch and need a cupful or so. But only the softer grains will grind to flour and never quite as fine as a mill grinds. The harder grains will only grind so fine and no finer no matter how long the blender runs.

When you use it to make pancakes etc. from whole grain, you add the rest of the recipe right away and bake the batter right away. Here, there is an advantage of fresh grinding the grain to a flour, because it is in small batches and used immediately.

DELICIOUS SIMPLE WHOLE RYE
STEAMED BREAD

Blender-chop 2 cups whole rye. Keep pushing in center on top to make sure all grain gets chopped. When all has gone down and passed through blades, pour into bowl and add:

 2 cups water
 ¼ cup molasses and ¼ cup honey, OR
 ⅓ cup honey alone
 pinch of salt (optional)

Pour into small loaf pan, about three-quarters full or into cans if you want a round loaf. Steam in large kettle in which you have covered the bottom with water. Place the pan on a wire rack or jar lids—or anything to hold it above the water. Cover and steam until all liquid is absorbed and the loaf is solid—about 1 to 1½ hours. Unmold.

This is delicious served with a slice of cheese or cream cheese, or any kind of cheese spread on it. Slice carefully, only after it has cooled through and through. Keep wrapped. This is a personal favorite of mine.

DAIRYLESS CREAMS AND TOPPINGS

I suppose this could be a new concept in cooking. Everyone seems to love the flavor of dairy products. Some people cannot eat them, some don't want to because of evidence against it. Some of the dairy products can be expensive, or you just might not have some on hand when you need them. Most of the dairy flavor can be duplicated quite well with products from the kitchen. Here again, in these dairyless recipes you will be using the oils raw, the egg yolks raw and in some cases fruits and other good ingredients that stay raw. I hope you like these. They taste good, but of course they won't always act like the real thing does. But, if you don't say anything, they'll be accepted as a dairy product. I started this dairy imitating with Part I and it is a personal satisfaction to bring you more, because this took a lot of experimenting and failures. I know that I'll be working on this thing for many years always trying to improve the originals.

DREAMING OF CREAM?

If you grew up on a farm, chances are that you ate spring lettuce with chopped dill, diced onion greens, seasoning and slightly sour cream. If the cream was sweet a few drops of vinegar were added to it. This salad was delicious piled on top of cooked new potatoes. Later in the summer, large cucumbers were peeled and sliced and served in the same way, usually with a little cut-up onion, seasoning and cream. But times are changing even down on the farm. Try these "cream" substitutes.

149

BASIC SOUR CREAM
(for using as a dressing)

In blender:

    1 cup near hot water
    1 tablespoon gelatin

Turn blender on and blend gelatin in, add:

    2 egg yolks
    ½ cup oil
    1 tablespoon vinegar
    1 teaspoon each honey and vege-sal or other sea-
      soning

This is ready to use as is over cucumbers or lettuce as mentioned above or for your favorite use of sour cream. Keeps a long time in the refrigerator and it sets like gelatin. To reuse add a little water and blend it smooth either with a fork or in the blender. To use as plain cream leave out the vinegar and use only a dash of salt.

PLAIN CREAM

For a cream base that won't get stiff in your refrigerator make it with cooked brown rice.

In blender:

    1 cup of cooked rice
    2 cups of water
    ½ cup of oil
    2 egg yolks or one cooked egg

This is bland flavored, but ready to use as cream in your recipes. Add to it the flavors that you want for the dish that you are using it in. Go by taste and add a bit of vinegar, seasoning, honey, until it's suitable to your use of it. Add more rice to make it thicker if desired.

These creams are not meant to be used in baked goods that call for cream. I have never tried them for this. They are meant for dressings, dips and things of that nature. They are also good for a meat dish which calls for sauteing the meat with cream. Flavor to taste

150

with vinegar, a dab of honey and seasoning before pouring over meat.

WHIPPED CREAM TOPPING

In blender:
    ½ cup hot water
    1 tablespoon gelatin
Turn blender on and blend gelatin in and add:
    2 egg yolks
    ½ cup oil
Put this in the refrigerator to set. This can be made far in advance or kept on hand to be used when needed. *When ready to use* beat the 2 egg whites very stiff and add:
    1 teaspoon vanilla
    ½ cup raw sugar
and beat stiff again. Then take the beaters and beat the stiff gelatin smooth. Pour the gelatin mixture over the egg whites and fold in by hand. Do not use the blender and mixer here as it takes the air out of the egg whites. This will last for hours at room temperature and hold up. Or refrigerate it to serve cold and if you freeze it, serve it for ice cream.

HONEY WHIPPED CREAM TOPPING

Follow the same recipe as for sugar, only add ⅓ cup honey to the stiff gelatin mixture before beating it smooth and adding it to the egg whites. A dash of almond flavoring can be added when using honey. If for some reason you don't want to use raw egg yolks, cook them in the amount of water called for in the recipe, but try and eat them raw whenever possible, as that is one thing that all health magazines agree on. They all advocate eating raw foods as much as possible.

MOCHA TOPPING

Use ½ cup hot coffee in place of the ½ cup of water at the beginning of the recipe.

These creams will be dairy-like in with foods but not suitable for a coffee cream. I have tried every way possible but have not been able to develop it for that, nor have I been able to come up with a margarine made with ingredients from the kitchen that has been satisfactory.

BUTTER AND JELLY SPREAD
(dairyless)

Soak 1 tablespoon plain gelatin in ½ cup of oil. Put in blender and add 1 egg and ½ cup honey. Blend well, add 1 cup of dried fruit such as apricots. This blends very thick so help along on the top.

DAIRYLESS MILK SHAKES AND ICE CREAMS

This is something I should never have started, because in summer my gang puts too great a demand on me to keep making them constantly. They can be made sweet with sugar or honey. We use honey almost exclusively. The honey in your area and the flavor of it will make a difference in the flavor of your milk shakes. You will notice a difference too, if you are used to the sweet-salt combination of commercial ice creams. They are actually oversweet because salt is added to everything and more sugar to overcome the salt. This cuts the cost of producing foods as it covers cheap ingredients with the salt-sweet combination. At home we can add fresh fruits and appreciate true flavor. Again here, if you won't tell, it will pass as a dairy milk shake and if you do want to use milk, freeze milk into ice cubes and use milk cubes instead of ice. Or use a sunflower seed or nut milk. Here again I worked out many recipes and ways, but finally settled on this one basic recipe. Any or all variations can be made from it.

DAIRYLESS MILK SHAKES USING FROZEN SWEETENED FRUIT
(thawed only enough to get it out of the package and broken up)

In blender:
   1 whole egg or two egg yolks
   ½ cup honey
   ½ cup oil
   1 teaspoon vanilla

Blend well and add approximately 1 cup of frozen pre-sweetened fruit and approximately 1 tray of ice cubes. By using frozen fruit it will get very thick, almost like ice cream, so help turn on the top to make it easier for the blender and to help all the ice and frozen fruit to blend well. Can be gotten thick enough to eat with the spoon like ice cream.

Strawberry is the smoothest and tastiest. Raspberry has the fine seeds in it, but is also very good.

MILK SHAKES USING ANY FRESH FRUIT
(or unsweetened frozen fruit)

   1 egg or 2 egg yolks
   ¾ cup honey
   ½ cup oil
   1 teaspoon of vanilla

Blend well and add:
   1 cup fruit
      Approximately 1 tray of ice cubes or until thick

Variations

Mocha—Freeze 1 tray of coffee into cubes and use for ice. Use ½ cup of honey. (This is a good way to use leftover cold coffee.)

Butterscotch—Use ½ cup dark raw sugar.

Carob—Add 3 tablespoons carob. Use ½ cup honey.

Maple Syrup—Have been fresh out for 2 years. Should be very good.

Fresh Peach—Use ¾ cup honey, ½ teaspoon almond flavoring and about 4 medium peaches.

Fresh Apricot—Same as peach using about 7 unpeeled, halved apricots.

Red Fruits—Cranberry, Strawberry, Raspberry—Use 1 cup unsweetened.

Dark Fruits such as ripe Gooseberries or Blueberries—Use 1½ cups of fresh fruit and vanilla flavoring. One of my favorites is blueberry.

Yellow and Orange Colored Fruits—Use 1 cup fresh fruit and almond flavoring, alone or with vanilla.

Papaya Juice—Use 1 cupful, in place of fruit.

MILK SHAKES USING GELATIN

Soften 1 tablespoon gelatin in ½ cup of cold water.

In blender:
   2 egg yolks
   ¾ cup honey
   ½ cup oil
   vanilla

Add the softened gelatin and blend well. Add about 2 cups of fresh strawberries, and about a cupful of ice to make it cold and thick. This will not get as thick as the other milk shakes as you won't be able to work as much ice in.

Variations

Carob—Carob milk shakes are the best made with gelatin. Use the same recipe using only ½ cup of honey, a tray of ice, and add 3 heaping tablespoons carob.

Other—All other flavors can be made with gelatin. Remember to use ½ cup of honey for frozen sweetened fruit and ¾ cup with fresh fruit.

The gelatin milk shakes are creamier and thicker, whereas without gelatin they are icier.

I have used ice in every brand of blender that I have worked with and do not find ice hard on blenders. BUT, do help along on the top as the mixture starts getting thick, because *that* is hard on the blender. You can use a spoon and help stir on the top. If you notice trouble, stop the blender and stir hard down to the bottom. It might be a piece of ice caught in an unusual way in the blades, which doesn't happen very often.

If you have a cheap blender and do feel that ice is too hard on it to put directly into the milk shake mixtures, you can fill the blender about ⅛ full of water and crush the ice in the water, then pour into a wire strainer and strain to add the ice to the milk shake. This however takes double the amount of ice cubes and the milk shakes won't get as thick. Blending ice cubes in water won't hurt any brand of blender. Crush the ice first, then make the milk shake.

These milk shakes can be made *ahead* of time and *frozen*. Set out ahead to soften before serving.

Berry-nut—A handful of nuts crushed and added makes tasty eating. If added to a *red* fruit such as cranberries, etc., it will taste like cherry nut ice cream. Try your own ideas, banana, what have you?

Here again is an example of how good nutrition can be packed into good eating. I have always been puzzled why people think that good eating is dull and tasteless. We find it just the opposite and I'm sure you will too.

MAKE AHEAD FROZEN SHERBETS
(dairyless)

ORANGE SHERBET

Separate 3 eggs

In blender:
> the 3 egg yolks
> 1 cup very hot water
> 1 tablespoon gelatin

Blend gelatin in and add:
> ½ cup honey
> ¼ cup oil
> 1 large can frozen orange juice

While the blender is melting the gelatin in the hot water, you have time to beat the 3 egg whites very stiff. Pour finished blender mixture over the egg whites and fold in by hand. Freeze.

FROZEN VANILLA DESSERT

In blender:
> 3 egg yolks
> 1 cup very hot water
> 1 tablespoon gelatin

Blend gelatin in well and add:
> ¾ cup oil
> ½ cup honey
> dash of vanilla

While gelatin is blending in beat the 3 egg whites very stiff and fold the blender mixture in when it is finished. Freeze.

Good served with fresh fruit on the top.

Raw apple sauce made with frozen orange juice is a very good topping for any of these milk shake recipes especially if they are vanilla flavored.

In most of my cooking I like to use just the egg yolks in the blender and save up the whites in the refrigerator. They make any dessert so elegant by making a stiff meringue with either sugar or honey and baking it on a buttered sheet or waxed paper and transferring them onto the dessert when serving it. Best baked in individual piles, piled high and put on individual desserts.

I'll repeat here that if you are not a user of honey, sugar can be used in place of it in any recipe in this book.

QUICK FRESH FRUIT TOPPING

    ⅛ cup juice (such as pineapple)
    1 box pectin
    1 container frozen fruit (1½ cups)

If fruit is unsweetened, add honey to taste when blending. Frozen strawberries or raspberries are real good as well as using any frozen concentrate.

FLOATING ORANGE ISLANDS ON PURPLE

In blender:
    1 cup very warm water
    3 tablespoons gelatin

Blend until high and white and add:
    1 can frozen orange juice

Spoon large pieces in dessert dishes. Pour cold unsweetened bottled grape juice over. Serve.

DAIRYLIKE DIP
(for chips or dipping)

Base (in blender):

> 2 hard cooked eggs
> 1 cup water (or cook the eggs in the cup of water)
> 1 cup cooked brown rice
> 1 tablespoon each of cider vinegar and honey
> 2 teaspoons of your favorite seasoning

Blend until very smooth. Ingredients can be hot or cold. When smooth add 1 cup oil and blend in.

Pour into bowl and flavor to your taste with whatever are your favorites. Use any instant soup mix (supermarket or from a health outlet), meat and tiny vegetable pieces such as celery, parsley, pickle bits, etc.

CAROB MILK SHAKE WITH BROWN RICE
(good for a summer treat frozen in cups or paper cups)

Put ¾ cup cold water in saucepan, sprinkle on 1 tablespoon gelatin, add 2 eggs and cook, stirring all the while until creamy looking.

Put this hot mixture into blender with ¾ cup of cold cooked brown rice. While blending add:

> ½ cup oil
> 3 full tablespoons honey (swirled on)
> 3 full tablespoons carob
> 1 teaspoon pure vanilla

Blend thick and start adding ice cubes, pushing them down if necessary and help along on top. Add ice cubes until blender is full or mixture is thick and icy. Ready to eat or to freeze in cups. If rice is hot, add gelatin and eggs and ¾ cup hot water to blender and omit cooking it.

HOME MADE ICE CREAM
DAIRYLESS

Set 2 cups of water on stove to boil. Blend 6 eggs and pour into the boiling water. Cook and return them to blender, one half at a time. To each half, add 1 cup sugar or ½ cup honey, and 1 cup oil. When blended smooth, pour into freezer. Fix the other half the same way. Add ½ gallon of the rice Magic Mix milk. Flavor to taste with vanilla and almond. Freeze in crank freezer. I fooled guests completely with this one. They said home made ice cream is always better.

Dairyless No. 2

This one also fooled my family completely. Follow same recipe using Magic Milk No. 1. I added a can of pineapple to it before freezing.

You can also use the Magic Milk made with seeds, but my gang here did not like it.

Find blender milk shakes under Nuts, Seeds, and Coconut.

DAIRYLESS ICE CREAM
(for crank type freezers)

Ingredients (makes one gallon)
   ½ gallon of water
   1 cup uncooked brown rice
   8 eggs
   3 cups light raw sugar or 2½ cups honey
   2 cups mild tasting oil, such as corn oil
   1 tablespoon plain gelatin
   2 to 3 tablespoons vanilla
   1 teaspoon almond

Method

1. Cook the cupful of brown rice in 1 quart of the water until very fluffed.

2. Blend the 8 eggs and stir into the hot rice when it's done.

3. You'll have to divide this in about 4 portions to do the blending. Put about ¼ of the cooked rice and egg mixture into the blender.

4. Add ½ cup of oil, part of the sugar to each batch letting it blend thick and adding from the remainder quart of water as necessary.

5. Repeat this 4 times until all the rice, egg mixture, the 2 cups of oil and the 3 cups of sugar has been blended as smooth as possible, adding the flavorings and the gelatin to one of the batches.

6. Add the remaining quart of water to the blender mixtures or the ice cream container, remembering that you used 1 quart to cook the rice.

7. Pour each batch directly into the ice cream container after blending and stir to mix well after all is blended.

8. Start the blender on LO very carefully as the hot mixture likes to go over the top.

This can be frozen immediately or cooled first. To be sure of a good freeze in a hand cranked ice cream use plenty of salt. If you can buy a livestock salt from a feed store, it will be cheap and will last for many years. It's the salt on the ice that releases the cold and makes for fast freezing.

Variations

Fruit such as strawberries, cherries and pineapple, or nuts can be added to make any flavor you want. Use at least 2 or more cups of fruit.

If it is made with honey, the addition of fruit makes it better. If it is made with sugar, the fruit is better served over the top. Raw jellies and purees make good ice cream toppings.

Carob—our kids like to sprinkle the carob powder on the ice cream plain, rather than making a syrup or freezing it in. If it's lumpy they even like it better.

This dairyless ice cream is much better if it's frozen hard in the electric freezer, or in our area set outside in the winter, after cranking. It scoops nicely with an ice cream scoop and makes nice banana splits, etc., if good and frozen.

On the contrary, the freezer ice cream made with dairy products on Pages 66 and 67 is the best eaten as soon as the freezer is opened after cranking. This freezes very hard after being put into a freezer. Set them both out for awhile before serving.

ABOUT THE RICE

You will notice a slight coarseness on your tongue from the rice, which has been guessed as being coconut added. If you want a very smooth ice cream to really fool, blend the rice with all the water after cooking and strain thru a wire strainer. Heat it and start with the eggs, etc., and the rest of the recipe. It really isn't necessary at all especially if you serve it with a topping or fruit, but on a certain occasion you might want to strain it.

This ice cream can be frozen without cranking altho it won't fluff as much. The gelatin can also be omitted.

OILS

The mildest flavored cold pressed oils for milk shakes and ice cream are:

    sesame
    soybean
    peanut
    corn
Two more oils that I buy are:
    safflower
    olive (rarely)
    sunflower

These three are stronger in flavor. Olive oil my family cannot seem to get used to. I might start a headache among store owners selling these, but I buy mine from a kind dealer who, when I order 2 gallons of each kind, only charges 10% over his cost. This supply lasts a long time and brings the cost down of a higher quality product. So the last years I haven't had too much experience with supermarket oils, except when demonstrating. I do know that corn oil is mild flavored wherever it's bought, but peanut oil is mild only if the label states that it's cold pressed. (For use in ice cream, etc.)

Dr. William Ellis of Tarentum, Pa., puts the oils, best in order, in his booklet in this way:

1. Sesame oil
2. Flaxseed oil
3. Safflower oil
4. Peanut oil
5. Soybean oil
6. Cottonseed oil
7. Olive oil
8. Corn oil

BLENDER DRINKS

This is a blender demonstrator's baby, and if a poll could be taken among blender owners, I'll bet this is the one use of the blender that would be the favorite.

You may have watched a blender demonstration where everything under the sun was thrown in and blended to a drink and to top it all, the mixture didn't even go over the top with the blender lid off! But, when trying it at home you found yourself washing down the cabinets, ceilings and walls? I have three different brands of blenders in my kitchen right now, and granted some don't go over the top as easily as others, I can assure you that they all will if conditions are right. But with a layer of food such as cabbage lying on top of the liquid, they won't go over the top. Always start with SLOW speed, THEN turn it up!

Now, to get a smooth emulsion of the ingredients that you are blending, there are a few things to know.

First of course is to start with the liquid you want to use. This is your choice on what you like or want. Use from this list or come up with your own.

    Unsweetened canned or frozen pineapple juice
    Canned juices of any kind
    Canned tomatoes
    V-8 canned juice
    Papaya
    Bottled juices
    Coconut milk
    Make your own nut and seed milks by blending
        them with water.
    Thawed frozen juices
    Cider

Fill the blender about ¼ full of juice or liquid. Let's say that you are using pineapple juice, which is one of the best. Now put on a layer of something soft like cabbage pieces, then add pieces of carrot, pieces of beet, pieces of apple and blend. To get it as smooth as possible, keep it thick. When everything you want to add seems to be as smooth as possible, add a banana and some ice cubes, also more pineapple juice if it's getting too thick.

Now, I never use recipes here for simple reasons, one being you seldom have on hand everything the recipe might call for, another is that once you start making these, you're only going to use what you want in your drink or shake anyway. So here is a list of ingredients that can be thrown in a juice and following that, some pointers on success with drink or shake blending.

Any fresh vegetables of any kind (carrots, celery, beets, cabbage, asparagus, etc.)

Any fresh fruits of any kind (bananas, apples, oranges, peaches, grapes, etc.)

Any nuts or seeds of any kind (walnuts, pecans, sunflower, pumpkin, etc.)

Any dried fruits of any kind (dates, raisins, apricots, etc.)

Fruits and vegetables only need washing and cutting up; no peeling is necessary. Celery will blend smooth including strings. Nuts and seeds will blend smooth. If using a hot broth, any vegetable or pieces of cooked meats can be added. (The exception is raw potato: You can add some, but too much gives an odd flavor.) Watch hot liquids; they go over the top easier.

To get the smoothest possible drink follow a procedure something like this: Start with the blender about ¼ or ⅓ full of juice. Cut the vegetables and fruits into chunks and keep adding them preferably while the blender is running. (This might save you getting a chunk of something hard, like a carrot, stuck in the blades.) Keep the mixture thick, add more juice as it thickens. Now the very last thing to add for smoothness is either a banana or ice cubes or both. Both will make the mixture smooth out. Ice also cools the drink and makes it more appetizing. Pour into serving pitcher and thin with juice to taste.

In these drinks, you can drink what you might not eat otherwise. Or you can drink a whole meal having the vegetables and fruits raw, but still complete as they grew.

Raw beets in combination with pineapple juice taste and look strawberry-like.

OUR FAVORITE

1 can of unsweetened pineapple juice (start with
   ¼ blender and keep adding as necessary)
1 beet or 2 or 3 smaller ones, cut up
1 large carrot or more smaller ones, cut up
1 or 2 Jerusalem artichokes
   pieces of celery, parsley, etc.
1 banana and ice cubes

This is typical of how I make them. They are never
made twice the same. I use what's around here or whatever the garden produced an over abundance of. It's
sweet enough with pineapple juice and banana but add
raw sugar or honey if you want.

Recently I've been reading about the nutrition in
wheat grass. This is one of the easiest things to grow
on the windowsill. Just plant wheat in a can or container and in a few days you have nice green grass to use in
a blender drink. You don't even know it's there and you
have good fresh vitamins and enzymes in the middle of
the winter.

You can add a whole egg, shell and all to these
drinks. I have tried whole eggs over and over again in
different ways in the blender and just can't get to
liking it. You will always have the fine grittiness either
on your tongue, or in the case of a blender drink, you'll
find it on the bottom of your glass. But, try them yourself and see if you like it. It's far easier to disguise bone
meal or dolomite powder in any baked goods, gravy or
puddings, than to spoil your family's taste for these
drinks. After all in these drinks you have a way to get
them to eat raw carrots, beets and other things they
might not touch otherwise.

As I've said before, anything can be added such as
dried fruits, etc. But, the case in this house is that any
fruit, fresh or dried, gets eaten so fast, that I just don't
add them to any drink. I like to add the carrots and
beets and things of that nature that move slower here.

An easy *Sunday supper* is hamburgers and a pineapple vegetable blender drink.

A GOOD TASTING SHAKE

¼ blender full of pineapple juice
2 or 3 carrots, cut up
   piece of beet
   handful of sunflower and pumpkin seeds
1 apple cored and quartered
   a dab of honey
   ice cubes

Blend until thick. Thin with more juice if wanted.

INSTANT SOUPS

Use any hot broth and add your raw vegetables. Chop or blend as fine as you like, and thin with more hot broth to taste, also season to taste with your favorite vegetable seasoning. This keeps your vegetables raw, but has a cooked taste and consistency. (Parsley is almost a must for good flavor in this kind of soup.)

FLAVOR GRAVY

There are two ways for making gravy with blended vegetables. If you want to keep the vegetables raw, make your gravy from your meat drippings very thick. Then chop or blend your vegetables fine either in water or in meat broth and stir into the hot, very thick gravy to the right consistency. Serve immediately without added cooking.

Cooked—Blend your vegetables in water or meat broth adding to the blender, a tablespoon of corn starch for every cup of gravy you plan to make. Pour into the hot meat drippings or boiling broth and keep stirring until thick.

Starchless Gravy—If you have a good rich meat dripping or broth, just blend it thick with vegetables and

166

serve as is for gravy. In these gravies as well as the soup, parsley added along with the other vegetables gives good flavor.

GELATIN FROM BLENDER JUICES

Any juice combination that you find you like in the blender can be made into gelatin. Or if you have some of this juice left over after a meal with vegetables and fruits blended in, don't throw it away. Take either a cupful of cold water or juice and sprinkle a tablespoon of gelatin over the top of it in a saucepan, for every pint of blended juice you have. Let it melt over a low heat and add to the juice. For a fruitier salad, cut banana and apple slices into the gelatin before you refrigerate it. Add nuts, canned pineapple or canned fruits and more honey or sugar if needed. About the only precaution needed here is to be sure to add enough gelatin for the amount of juice and fruits, to set it stiff.

CRANBERRY FRUIT GELATIN SURPRISE
(the surprise is the vegetables hidden in it)

In blender:

 1½ cups of pineapple juice
 2 small beets
 1 small carrot

Blend very fine on hi speed. Pour either in bowl or cake pan. Put another cup of juice in the blender and chop 1½ cups of cranberries, honey or sugar added to taste (¼ to ½ cup) (add a handful of walnuts here if you want to and chop). Pour in with the rest of the mixture and add 1 can of crushed or pineapple chunks. (2 cups or more with juice) Now, sprinkle 4 heaping tablespoons of plain gelatin on a cup of pineapple juice and when it has soaked in, melt it over medium heat, stirring till it's melted, and add to the bowl of blended ingredients. Pour into mold or cake pan and cut apple slices and banana slices over the top. Press down some so

167

juice covers them to keep them from turning dark. A Marshmello layer could be put on top (see Cranberries section for making the Marshmello part).

Now, that is an example of making gelatin with vegetables disguised in it. Any vegetable could be blended or chopped in. Lettuce in fine pieces is good. Try anything! About the only rule needed is to keep tasting so the taste remains good. Don't overdo it with the vegetables that aren't liked at your house, so no one will catch on.

Another way to be successful with this is to use the fruits you know are liked in these gelatin salads to mask and hide the rest. There is something else useful here and that is, after you have been serving things they wouldn't eat before in some of the sneaky ideas I've been giving in this book, for some time, and they still say they don't like this or that, you can tell them that they've been eating it all along. If they are mature enough, they just might think, well if that's the case I can eat them in any form or way from now on.

MAKE YOUR OWN V-8 JUICE

In blender:
>   2 cups canned tomatoes
>   ½ cup carrot pieces
>   ½ to ¾ cup celery pieces or tops
>   wedge of lettuce
>   piece of cabbage
>   piece of onion or onion top
>   1 teaspoon of vegetable seasoning
>   some good sized sprigs of parsley
>   piece of sweet red or green pepper

Blend until smooth and thick. Add ice cubes at the end to cool it and make it smoother.

The taste is similar to the canned V-8 juice you buy. If you would like to add other fresh vegetables, experiment with the vegetables available to you.

The color of this changes as to the amount of green vegetables you add. It will be a darker red than what you are used to, if you add beets.

GARDEN BLENDER DRINKS

If you have owned a blender for any length of time, chances are that you have made drinks similar to this from the products in your garden or area.

RHUBARB

Fill blender ½ full of water. Add cut-up fresh (or frozen), unpeeled rhubarb pieces. Pour through medium fine strainer. Use a rubber spatula to press the rhubarb pulp dry. Add more water if necessary, honey and ice to taste. Good added to lemonade too.

PEPPERMINT

Any variety of the mints that grow in your yard make a good drink. In the blender either hot or cold water can be used, as the chopping releases the flavor. Add a handful of peppermint and blend well and fine. Pour through a wire strainer, pressing the juice out of the pulp with a rubber scraper. Add honey and ice to taste.

Peppermint and rhubarb drinks are good mixed together. Fresh fruit such as raspberries or strawberries are good blended in.

BLUEBERRY OR RIPE GOOSEBERRY DRINKS

In blender:
    1½ cups of any berries
    ½ cup of honey
Blend with 1 cup of water and strain through wire strainer. Makes a ½ gallon of nectar drink. Put the

strained peelings and seeds in jar covered with water in refrigerator. They still have some pep in them, and the water can be strained out and added to another drink.

ICES OR WHIZZES

A GOOD ICE

    1 can frozen cranberry juice
    1 can frozen pineapple-orange juice
    1 cup rhubarb pieces
    ½ cup water
    2 tablespoons papaya concentrate

Add ice until good and icy. Serve.

CARNIVAL ICE

Fill blender ½ full of water. Add a tray of ice cubes and blend until ice is all shattered and smooth. Strain through wire strainer. Put ice into cups and pour favorite frozen or fresh fruit concentrates over it.

GRAPE ICE

Have you ever had to restrain your children at a fair on a hot day to keep them from those colored ices? They look so tempting and are one of the biggest money makers the peddlers ever came up with. A shot of sugar syrup, artificially sweetened, highly colored, and a mound of crushed ice. All this you get for only 15 or 20 cents! Well, make them at home often enough and they won't tempt the kids so much.

Keep plenty of ice cubes on hand. Put a handful in the blender. Add pure grape juice. Blend until ice is fine. It takes one can of frozen grape juice to make one blender full. Keep adding ice cubes until the blender is full. You will be surprised how refreshing and good-tasting these are. They can be sipped slowly or eaten with a spoon.

Variation: This is something I have served guests often. Freeze milk into ice cubes. Set the trays out a little while before you blend them to give them a chance to thaw just a little bit. Put one can of frozen grape juice in the blender and blend while adding the milk cubes one by one. The finished product is eaten like an ice cream and when dished up is just like eating a sherbet—smooth and creamy. Grape juice must be thawed or liquefied before adding ice.

BLENDER WHIZZES

Blender Whizzes are nothing more than fresh fruits or fresh and canned fruits blended together. For example combine fresh pineapple, fresh strawberries, some mint leaves and honey or sugar to sweeten. Add ice if wanted. You can use combinations of watermelon, muskmelon, any green leaves, coconut and coconut milk, dates, any dried fruit and bananas, etc. These are mostly made of fruits. I don't make anything along this line, simply because fruit just does a disappearing act around here as it grows. I'm lucky to find a banana or apple when I want to put some into a salad.

WORKING WITH WATER IN THE BLENDER

Almost anything can be chopped in a liquid in the blender. Fill the blender about ½ full of juice or water and chop to the fineness desired. There are several factors here which make a difference: one is the size of your blender. Naturally the bigger capacity a blender has, the bigger the pieces that it can chop. Another is speed. The faster you run it the finer it chops in a very short time. A timer on a blender seems to me to be the utmost of uselessness. There are very few times that you can walk away from the blender because almost everything is done so fast. The next factor is the amount of liquid. The bigger the volume of liquid to the amount chopped, the nicer the chopped pieces will be.

USING JUICE

I have reached a point where I do almost all the vegetable chopping in a juice such as papaya with water or straight pineapple juice. That way it gives the strained vegetables more flavor and the strained juice is used on the table as a drink. Some of the vitamins and minerals are released into the juice and your kids will drink some even if they don't touch the vegetable.

CHOPPED BEETS AND CARROTS SALAD

A simple and quick salad is to use either washed, unpeeled raw beets or carrots either alone or in combination. First drain canned pineapple and add the juice from it to more pineapple juice. Chop the vegetables in the juice, strain the chopped vegetables out and mix them with the pineapple. Use the juice for a drink or punch. This gives you both a salad and a drink for your meal. Jerusalem artichokes are good this way too.

BEETS

Beets are easy to grow. I usually have a lot of them, but they are hard to serve raw. Other than pickling them, most people don't have much use for beets. Now, from all I've ever read about beets, they are considered tops for nutrition, but mainly if they are raw. Have you gotten your family to like raw beets? Beets used together with pineapple juice taste like strawberry. Junie, who is four years old, came to the table one day and said, "Oh goody, no Blah Beets." What she didn't know is that they were in the drink and in the cranberry salad and she didn't even come near realizing it. This same sneaky way can be used on kids older than 4 too.

Raw Beet Relish is on Page 121.

PICKLED BEET SLICES

Still like the flavor of pickled beets? Do it the easy way! Blend ½ cup honey and ½ vinegar and add 1 to 2 tablespoons of pickling spice. The spice can be left whole or blended in. Now slice raw, unpeeled, washed beets very thinly into this and let marinate in refrigerator until needed. They are crisp and good. More can be sliced in as you use them for a long time to absorb the flavor.

POTATO PANCAKES

Let's leave using beets for now and continue using the blender and water for chopping. I had recipes for potato pancakes in *Wheat and Sugar Free*. Then I got a letter from Eileen Oliver of Breckenridge, Pa., telling me how her mother used to grate the potatoes into water for potato pancakes. She wrote, "My mother used to grate potatoes into water, strain them, allow the starch to settle, then return the starch to the potatoes. Then she would add eggs, one for every medium potato, maybe a bit of onion and fry them in oil." Now I've tried this, in the blender and in water, and I really like it. The potato pancakes get very light and fluffy. You can leave the starch out and have fewer calories. The starch sinks to the bottom after the potatoes are strained and the water can be poured right off.

Once in a while Lanny has to be the chef for one reason or another. Potato pancakes are his specialty. He likes them best doing it the old fashioned way on a grater. But if I make them I like to use Eileen's way.

The line between chopping in a liquid and making a

blender drink can be pretty thin. In other words, if you have the blender running too fast and too long you might have to drink your salad.

QUICK AND EASY FRUIT SALAD IDEAS

Liquid vitamin C, available in health catalogues (not a drug store variety), makes a delicious, low calorie salad dressing for tossing fresh fruits. It adds a good flavor, some sweetness, and keeps the fruits from darkening. I tried it for freezing apples and it worked well, but have not used it on a large scale as yet for freezing.

Perhaps you like to use a can or jar of canned fruit with your fresh fruits in a fruit salad. I like to use the large pineapple chunks, juice and all. Then dry grind raw sunflower seeds and pumpkin seeds, either one alone or together, and use just enough to thicken the fruit salad. Stir them in last of all. Makes the fruit attractive, too.

Fresh fruits, dates, nuts and perhaps some canned fruit are very good mixed with sweet salad dressing (Pages 119 and 120). I've had cooks ask me if I mixed ice cream in my fruit salad when made this way.

I get carried away buying apples in large amounts, especially if they are local apples. I then have to connive every conceivable way to use them up fresh before they spoil. These are some of the ways they are used until they are gone.

Wash them and with drops of water still on them, put them into a clear bowl and have them sitting around at all times. They then look more appetizing this way and more are eaten whole.

For every meal, quarter them, cut out the cores and

174

arrange on a platter. There are always only a few that will take a whole apple, and apples cut into quarters with the cores left in are revolting, but almost everyone will gradually end up reaching for a quartered cored apple. If they are red or whatever color the skin is, it makes a very attractive plate with the creamy color apple and the colored skins. I almost always cut up a platter of apples for company lunch like this too. If there are kids, they'll just keep taking as they go by until they are gone.

For an appetizer tray preceding a dinner or where you like something special, dip the quarters into any of the following: (Use toothpicks for dipping and leave them in.)

Fresh Orange Juice, thawed.

Liquid Vitamin C (Good—different flavor).

Fresh Orange Dip—Wash and cut up a whole seedless orange, peel and all, or remove seeds. Throw orange pieces in the blender with ½ cup water, 1 tablespoon honey, and blend very smooth. Dip apples in. If any of this dip is left over, it can be used in a raw jelly, or punch, or something like a marmalade, as it becomes thick in the refrigerator.

Then a lot of apples can be used up in making raw applesauces (see Pages 44 and 45), or raw fruit pies.

Last of all, if the apples are starting to really look tough, I'll resort to using them in some cooked form, such as applesauce or maybe a rare baked apple.

This same reasoning can be applied to any bargain in fruit that can be bought. There are more fresh fruit uses scattered throughout this book.

FRUIT PLATTER GALA

Stick toothpicks into the following:

Cut apples into quarters and remove the cores. Peel

seedless oranges thinly, leaving the white on. Cut into slices. Cut bananas into chunks. Stick with toothpicks and arrange all these on a platter. Over the top scatter: whole dates, large pieces of pineapple. This makes delicious tidbit eating, looks inviting and attractive, and is not limited to the above fruits. Any that are in season and not mushy could be used. Sticking the pieces with toothpicks is just for novelty and not necessary. It is surprising how fast children gobble up fruits and vegetables if they are presented right. We mothers and grandmothers can use our ingenuity just as well as the commercial manufacturers of chips and snacks. I never seem to have any trouble getting any plates empty. Children who are used to candy, pop, and commercial snacks really seem to go for wholesome snacks too when they are made with a little temptation added to sell them. There are other ways too, such as using one of these cutters that cuts everything wavy. They don't cost much and you push them through a carrot like a knife. Let your kids cut up some carrots with one, and you might not get too many to the table. They eat while they play, which is what your intentions were in the first place, and the more you scold and fuss that they shouldn't eat any, the more they sneak into their little faces.

___RAW FRUIT PIES

Surplus fruit can be used up this way or make them just for a treat. These really are good. I've never been too exact in my recipes here either but will tell you how I make mine.

The easiest and simplest is to use pineapple juice. Put it into a saucepan to get hot, keeping back about a ½ cup to mix the cornstarch in. Use a *heaping* tablespoon of cornstarch to every cup of liquid. Stir into the hot juice in the saucepan and keep stirring until very thick and bubbling. The idea is to have it extra thick. Now

176

cut your fresh fruit into this hot thickened mixture until it's heavy with fruit, and add extra honey or sugar if needed. Two egg yolks can be added to the hot mixture to give it more richness. Flavoring isn't necessary, but almond flavoring enhances fruit such as peaches and apricots.

If you don't have pineapple juice, make the same recipe as for lemon pie using water, cornstarch, egg yolks, and honey or sugar and lemon juice. But always make it very heavy so that it will be stiff after adding the fruit. If it's too stiff after the fruit, honey, etc., are all in, thin it with a little more juice. Or thin it with crushed pineapple, juice and all. Pineapple added to these fresh fruit pies is always good. A cupful or more of fruit can be crushed and added along with the sliced fruit. Turn this cooked mixture with the fresh fruit cut in, into your favorite crumb crust, or baked crust. Top with more crumbs and refrigerate.

MY CRUMB CRUST

In blender:
- 1 egg
- ¾ cup oil
- 1 teaspoon vanilla
- ¼ cup honey
- good pinch salt (optional)

Pour over 3 or 4 cups of rice flour. Stir and work with hands until nice and crumbly. Add more flour if necessary. Crumble into pie plate and pat up the sides with your fingers. Bake some loose in another pie plate to crumble over top of pie. Add cinnamon to crumble mixture for a variation, or when making fresh apple pie.

HARD CRUST

A hard crust that we like for using with pumpkin pie is the same recipe above, only leave out the honey or sugar and add a tablespoon of vinegar to the blender mixture. Pour over flour, get nice and crumbly and add a little water to hold it together. Press into pie plate and up the sides by hand. (Faster and easier than rolling out a crust.)

COOKED FRUIT SALAD DRESSINGS

Again the same principle can be used for a cooked fruit salad dressing. Cook a very thick sauce either with lemon juice or pineapple juice using egg yolks if you want to. Then cut in your fruits, add a can or so of canned fruit, juice and all, dates, nuts, etc. By this time it should be just right, but if it is too thick, thin with more juice or as my mother did years ago, with sweet cream. Sweeten to taste before you thin it.

RHUBARB PUDDING CAKE

Fill large pyrex cake pan about ½ full of cut up fresh or frozen rhubarb. Sprinkle ½ cup raisins over the top and sprinkle with cinnamon.
In blender:
    4 eggs
    2 cups honey
    1 cup oat (or other) flour
    1 tablespoon baking powder
      vanilla
Blend well, pour over rhubarb, and bake at 350° until brown and bubbly.

RHUBARB SAUCE

Cook rhubarb, raisins and sweeten with honey. When all cooked soft, add tapioca until thick. Leave on LO heat until tapioca is soft. Add cinnamon after done cooking. Regulate the thickness of this by the amount of tapioca you add. Good served with meat.

CRANBERRIES

There are many cranberry recipes, most of them calling for cooked cranberries. Here we will just work on using them raw. I suppose the old combination of oranges and cranberries is the favorite. One morning, when I was demonstrating blenders, I was going to make a cranberry, orange marshmello salad. The counter was high and I couldn't see into the blender. The orange was a dry one and didn't want to chop decently. I didn't have enough cranberries in the blender and I was pushing them down with the rubber scraper and hacked it all up. Then for some reason one of the blender's blades wouldn't move no matter what I tried. It was early and there was only one woman watching me. But in spite of all the goofs, she went right up and bought a blender. After she left, I tried the blender jar again where the blades wouldn't move and it worked perfectly. It never gave me any trouble again. This is the way it was made.

CRANBERRY MARSHMELLO SALAD

First chop 1½ cups of fresh or frozen cranberries in the blender and put in bowl. Next wash one or two unpeeled, seedless oranges and cut up. Throw into the blender and add ½ cup honey. Chop. Mix with chopped cranberries. Now this can be served as relish alone or with nuts, etc., sweetened to taste.

MARSHMELLO PART

In blender:
  1 cup very warm or hot water
  2 tablespoons gelatin—blend well
Add:
  ½ cup oil
  ½ cup honey or sugar
  1 teaspoon vanilla and ¼ teaspoon almond or 1 tablespoon orange extract

Add ice cubes to thicken it and when you see that it's starting to get thick or when the jar starts feeling cold, turn it out into a bowl. Pour the cranberry orange relish over and fold in slowly and carefully. For a 3 colored effect, fold in the chopped cranberries and chopped oranges separately.

PINK CRANBERRY

Make the same, only add the orange and cranberries right to the running blender. Then add the ice to thicken it. If the cranberries are frozen it will thicken without ice and have a richer flavor.

ORANGE MARSHMELLO

A can of frozen unthawed orange juice can be used in place of the oranges, but add it to the marshmello part instead of the cranberries. Try this orange marshmello in any salad. Good with carrot and pineapple salad too.

MY FAVORITE WAY OF SERVING CRANBERRIES

I like to use the same cranberries twice! Once in the punch and again in the salad!

APPLE CRANBERRY PUNCH

In blender:
  1½ cups either fresh or frozen cranberries
  ½ cup honey
  1 cup water

Let blend until thick and smooth. Add 1 unpeeled, quartered, cored apple. Blend and strain through wire strainer, shaking and stirring the mixture to keep it straining. Don't rub it through the strainer too hard in order to keep the punch clearer.

Add enough water to make about a quart of punch. This will still be strong enough to be able to add ice to the punch bowl. Repeat and make as many batches as you need for your punch bowl.

Now, here again you can serve this strained cranberry as a relish either alone or dolled up with nuts, grapes, pineapple, etc.

CRANMELLO

Make the Marshmello Part from the Cranberry Marshmello Salad. When it's getting thick or is real thick, add the strained relish from the punch. If you want the colors to be white and red, stir carefully. If you like it pink stir the relish in hard. You can use up to 4 or 5 batches of strained relish to one part of marshmello. But if you would like more marshmello in for the amount of relish you have, make another batch of marshmello to add to it. Doll this up with nuts, etc. too if wanted.

Fresh Grapes are always a good combination with cranberry.

Dried Apricots are real tasty with cranberry. If you don't like to use a citrus fruit like oranges, dried apricots will give about the same flavor.

APRICOT CRANBERRY SALAD

In blender:
- 1 cup very warm water
- 2 tablespoons gelatin

Blend well and long and add:
- ½ cup oil
- ½ cup honey or sugar
- 1 teaspoon vanilla and ¼ teaspoon almond flavoring
- 1½ cups cranberries, let blend fine
- 1 cup dried apricots, blend only to chop
- ½ cup nuts, turn only on and off to chop them
- 1 cup water or juice, blend in quickly or stir in

Pour into oblong cake pan and let set in refrigerator. The fruits will rise to the top and the bottom layer will have a creamy-like texture. Cut into bars.

Canned apricots or fresh apricots can be used too.

ABOUT BLENDING GELATIN

If you have a failure, such as your marshmello or gelatins made in the blender won't set, chances are that the gelatin didn't blend in enough to completely melt. It has to blend long, until you don't see the gelatin grains anymore. The hotter the water the faster it melts, but also it takes longer to set if you add ice cubes to the blender. The colder the water the longer you will have to run it to melt it in, but also it will take less ice to set it. Also if you used ice in the blender and want to make another marshmello batch, take into account that the blender jar is now cold and will cool the cup of water that you are using to blend the gelatin in. In this case use hotter water to start another batch.

When you add ice to a blender mixture, put your hand on the jar while it is blending. When the jar starts to feel cool, the gelatin is just next to setting. At this point you can still pour it out of the blender, but it will set right away anyhow. You will need less ice this way if you go by the cool touch on the blender jar.

RAW CRANBERRY JELL

This is good alone or mixed in with other jams or jellies.

In blender:

      1 cup honey, blend

Good honey will get very thick in the blender—(good way to make Fluffed Honey)

      1 box pectin
        blends very thick
      1½ cups frozen cranberries

Turn on and off and help push down to make it easier for the blender, until the cranberries are chopped. Refrigerate.

For a cooked-like textured jam, cook part of the cranberries with the honey and pectin and add the rest chopped and raw.

See also cranberry recipes on Page 62.

BEETS AND CRANBERRIES OR RED FRUITS

You can work a small carrot and 2 or 3 small beets into almost any cranberry relish or salad without detection. Even if your family eats raw vegetables, you can add a little more nourishment to these salads. Beets are hard to serve raw, even in a tossed salad. If too many beets are added to a salad it will turn the whole salad red. I have found with my family and with guests that beets are liked by very few, even if they are cooked. But with any red fruit such as raspberries or cranberries, you can add some and not have it noticed, if they are blended in or chopped in the blender before adding. This isn't true though, if the beets are cut into pieces. You have to blend them in a juice or chop into relish consistency before working them into a gelatin or fruit whiz or wherever you can manage to do it. Watch it and don't overdo it. If a member of your family despises beets and gets on to you, he might be suspicious of every red relish, gelatin or dish you serve!

HEN BLENDING

We had a situation this fall in this part of the country and I'm sure other places too, where farmers had no market for their stewing hens. They couldn't even give them away. Now these are chickens that can run and scratch and eat green grass and do things that chickens were created for. Instead, the supermarkets are selling stewing hens that never are allowed outside as old as they get. They are confined in cages or barns, and when their usefulness is over they become stewing hens. Their skin is nice and white and it lies in among the meats wrapped in cellophane. The stewing hens that grow up among us here have a golden yellow skin when dressed out, from the corn and things they eat that a good scratching will turn up. This is true of ducks, geese or any birds. But few persons still remain that know this and remember what good meat should taste like.

Regardless where you buy a stewing hen or old rooster, it is one of the best bargains of meat you can buy. Many families overlook the use of stewing hens because they don't know how good they are or how to begin to prepare one. A large old hen or rooster, when sliced nicely and spread out on a platter, can pass for turkey any day.

SIMPLICITY

We'll start simple and work up. In fact simple is the way to start with every chicken. Just throw it into a large tight covered pot, add approximately half as much water as chicken and cook slowly. If you clean your own chickens as I do, don't bother with cutting them

184

up. Freeze them whole and cook them whole with the giblets. If you are gone during the day and don't have time for any long cooking, set them on to cook during the evening while you are at home. I've set them on a low heat to cook while we were gone during the evening, and when we got home they were done. The length of cooking really isn't important. They are good just done or so well done that the meat falls off the bones. If they are real soft, you can lift the meat off with tongs and arrange it on the platter; if the meat is not too soft, it can be sliced with a sharp knife. After you arrange it on a platter, sprinkle it with a vegetable seasoning. It's good cold or hot this way. A cooked cold chicken in the refrigerator will keep for days and is always ready to use.

A real convenience is having cooked chicken on hand either in the refrigerator or freezer. You can bake a whole roaster full of chickens at 300° until very soft. Then cut up the meat and freeze it with a little of the broth. By the way, don't add any water or liquid to them if you roast them this way. When you need a fast meal or sandwich, heat through, and it's ready to serve.

THE BROTH

Oh what can be done with the broth! This is the best part.

SCRUMPTIOUS GRAVY

Follow cooking method above. Put 1 to 2 cups of broth in blender. Estimate approximate amount of broth remaining in kettle and measure 1 tablespoon of cornstarch into blender for each cup of gravy you are making. Blend and add to hot broth in kettle, stirring fast until thick. Season to taste with vegetable seasoning. Serve at once.

YOUR OWN SOUP CONCENTRATE

This is yellow with little green things in it, and with the blender, the vegetables stay raw with that same delicious cooked taste! Use one cup of broth in the blender and keep the rest hot on the stove.

In blender:

    1 cupful of hot chicken broth
       about ½ cup each carrot and celery pieces
       about ¼ cup of onion pieces and parsley
    1 teaspoon of seasoning such as vegetable seasoning
       a dash of ground allspice (optional)

Blend well and pour into soup bowl. Thin out with the remaining hot broth to taste. This unthinned soup also makes a good gravy and keeps the vegetables raw.

MY FAVORITE CHICKEN AND GRAVY

This chicken stew type of thing is elegant for a company dinner and you don't tire yourself making it. This has to be cooked, not baked, in your largest kettle.

Cook one or two stewing hens with half as much water as chicken. Cook until almost done—about 1½ hours. (This can be done ahead of time.) If chicken is done lift it out until the vegetables are cooked. About 45 minutes before serving time, add the following and cook in the broth.

    Whole washed unpeeled potatoes
    Whole small onions or large onion rings or cut up green onion tops
    Large celery pieces, celery tops or celery seeds
    One or two teaspoons of whole allspice
    Good sized carrot pieces or small carrots
    Cut up fresh parsley
    Pieces of red or green sweet pepper (optional)
    Vegetable seasoning and a pinch of peppercorns if you like them

Put vegetables in broth around chicken and cook all on low heat just until done. If chicken was lifted out during this time, return it for a while to reheat. To serve, get out your largest platter, tear the meat apart with tongs and arrange in the middle. Place the steamed vegetables around the meat. Soften one tablespoon of cornstarch for each cup of broth in a little cold water. Stir into the hot broth and cook until thick and clear. Spoon over the platter of meat and vegetables and serve the remainder in a gravy boat. The allspice and peppercorns will make the gravy attractive, although each person has to remove them. Garnish with fresh parsley sprigs, and maybe you'll hear "I never knew old chicken could taste so good!"

CHICKEN AND BROWN RICE

The cooking is the same. Add any or all the ingredients above except potatoes. About 45 minutes before chicken is done put the brown rice in the broth around the chicken and cook until done. Use either rice alone or in combination with vegetables.

CHICKEN VEGETABLE OR RICE SOUP

The method and ingredients are the same as the stew only cut the vegetables in smaller pieces. Lift out the chicken and cut part of it into small cubes and add.

DOUBLE ECONOMY

You can get two meals out of one chicken by using the chicken for one meal and the broth for another. Use the ideas given here or your own. Cold chicken, especially the breast, is good for school lunches sprinkled with vegetable seasoning.

A cold chicken platter is good for any party or meal, the appeal being in the way it's presented and arranged. Cubes cut about ½-inch square and put on toothpicks are good for dipping, including the giblets. Dairyless Dip on Page 158.

COOK WHILE YOU SLEEP

A large roaster full of chicken can bake during the night. If you bake only one, add a little water. If you bake more than one, they form their own liquid. If you go to bed late, start the oven when you put them in anywhere from 200 to 300 degrees. Or start them with the oven timer at about 3 or 4 in the morning. When it's time to get up or when you smell them, check on them to see if they are done. The meat can be removed from the bones and added to hot gravy made from the broth any time you want to use it.

COLD GELATIN CHICKEN LOAF

You probably have bought a cold meat in the meat department of your market called turkey loaf? Well make an even better one with a stewing hen. Sliced thin, it's got a clear gel with white and dark pieces of meat throughout it. Cook one chicken with giblets in 1 quart of water until soft and easily removed from the bones. When cool, remove from the bones, and discard the ribs, neck, etc., to avoid getting a fine bone in the loaf. Add 5 or 6 tablespoons plain gelatin to the cool broth and allow to soften. Heat only long enough to melt the gelatin. Lay the chicken meat and giblet pieces in strips the long way in a loaf pan or square freezer container. When you slice it, the pieces will cut crossways and form little cubes in the slice. Refrigerate until set hard. Don't bother to skim any fat off before it is set, as it all rises to the top and can be washed off the stiff loaf under the hot water faucet. Unmold the loaf and it is ready for slicing. Season to taste with vegetable seasoning.

CHICKEN LEGS
(the part that is walked on)

I have never been able to eat a cooked chicken leg due only to their unattractive appearance. Some people like them. But they are almost pure gelatin and if you should ever find yourself in possession of some, cook them and use the broth. The broth gets stiff after it's cooled and is good to add to something like the chicken loaf above or any chicken dish. I always cook them along with chicken if I have some and then discard them if no one wants to eat them.

ORANGE DUCK

Pour one large can of frozen orange juice over duck in deep stainless steel waterless kettle. Dice one onion and sprinkle over duck. Sprinkle over all this one teaspoon seasoning salt. Cover tightly and start on medium heat, turning duck once in awhile to brown it evenly. When brown, turn to low heat and finish cooking. Time required depends on size of duck—from one to three hours. Use the browned juice for gravy on mashed potatoes.

FAMILY FAVORITES

TOP HAT SANDWICHES

These are sandwiches where the dough and filling is baked together. I'm sure that any flour can be used in them if you want to substitute. Ingredients needed for 2 dozen sandwiches are:

2 pounds hamburger
1 quart sauerkraut
1 fresh or canned pimento
2 or 3 dill pickles
2 or 3 large onions (Cut into ½ inch slices. Separate the rings and use the inside small rings in the relish part.)
basil flakes

Relish Part for Sandwich Filling

Put ½ of the sauerkraut in the blender and chop relish-like. Pour into a wire strainer and chop the second half the same way. Return the strained sauerkraut juice to the blender and chop the pickles. Strain and repeat, chopping the pimento. If it's a canned pimento turn on and off only once very quickly, or it'll be a mush. Put the sauerkraut juice back in once more to chop the onions. Use only the centers and save the outside rings for shaping the sandwiches. Now leave all this relish in the strainer to strain while the dough is made.

Dough

3 eggs separated; yolks in the blender and whites in large bowl
1 cup of the strained sauerkraut juice
1½ cups of rice, oat, and soy flours mixed (½ cup of each)
½ cup oil

Blend well. Beat egg whites very stiff with mixer. Sprinkle 1 tablespoon of baking powder over them and beat once more until high and creamy. Pour blender mix over the egg whites and fold in by hand.

Putting Top Hats Together

Place onion rings on oiled cookie sheet. Fill ½ full of dough, sprinkle each with basil flakes and crumbled raw

190

hamburger. Sprinkle heavily with the relish mix. Then put a dab of dough on top of all this and bake at 350° for about 30 minutes or until the tops are lightly browned. Serve hot or cold.

Pizza Type

For a quick method spread all the dough in a large cake pan. Sprinkle with basil, then crumbled hamburger, then with the relish, and bake at 350° for half an hour. Cut into serving pieces.

STEARMN

That's a German name for this dish and so help me I tried my best to spell it the way it sounds. This is a pancake-type sort of thing or one of the many flour-type things that the ladies used to like to fix. It originally was always made with white wheat flour, but I find it can be made with almost any flour although it loses something and isn't quite the same. I usually use brown rice or oat flour. The blender really makes these fast and simple to make. Put enough oil in skillet to cover the bottom generously to get hot while you fix the batter in the blender.

Batter

6 eggs
1 cup milk
1½ cups flour
pinch salt

Blend and add about 2 more cups of milk.

Pour into the hot skillet all at once. Some of the oil will rise to the top. Let the bottom brown well and turn over with spatula in big chunks. Always let the bottom brown well and don't turn over too much, at least at first. If you get this fine and crumbly, it's spoiled. The batter has to brown in chunks or good-sized pieces.

When it's all cooked through, it's ready to serve, and actually doesn't take long. Keep the skillet uncovered.

This can be eaten with a meal as is or with a little syrup or honey. They are good with eggs or a little sausage or meat.

This Stearmn recipe brought letters from cooks that I can include now in this revised edition of the book. It would seem that different nationalities made this dish and thought it native to their country. I was brought up to believe that it was German. A letter from Mrs. Mary Theiner of Waukegan, Illinois, tells me that she is Austrian-born and this dish is Austrian and named after the Emperor (Kaiser) Franz Josef of Austria. It was named after him and called *Kaiser Schmarren* and served with powdered sugar and thick raspberry jelly. Her mother made it in a lot of butter. Then, very interestingly, Mrs. Marie Heeren of Akron, Iowa, wrote me that she bakes it in the oven and they have always called it Unapankaka. Also, we ordered Swedish pancakes once in a restaurant and they turned out to be this recipe.

Here the kids, when they were little, dubbed them "thin pancakes." The kids really like these large thin pancakes. Use the same recipe, only fix them in a pan by melting a pat of butter in the pan, pouring in a dab of batter, and lifting the pan to make the batter spread out real thin. Turn over, when pancake looks set, to brown for a minute or so on the other side. If you have the pan hot and the heat quite high, you can really clip along making these. They get good with whole wheat flour; and I put a little bone meal and wheat germ in each batch.

For our family of 6, it takes two batches, which are made all at once and poured together. Stir each time before pouring batter into pan as the flour settles and the last pancakes will be too heavy. It is surprising the difference the same recipe can make, fixing it either as "Stearmn" or "thin pancakes."

IDEA EXCHANGE

Since my recipes have been published in *Prevention*, I have gotten a lot of wonderful letters from cooks and mothers all over the country. They point out one obvious fact. That is, we can read and we also know what is good for our families. But no matter how enthusiastic or glowing the accounts are of good food and products, they won't get people to eat them, unless they taste good. Now, it's true that most of the recipes printed that are "good" for you, don't taste good. I personally don't think that good food has to be forced down just because we think we should eat this or that. I believe that good food should taste good and that it *can* taste good without artificial flavors and colors. We know what our children do like and will eat, so we can disguise things they don't like in the flavors they do, by not putting too much in to take away the dominating flavor that they like.

Then we don't have to buy certain products or can buy a better one in place of the inferior one. Take potatoes for example: Anyone knows unpeeled fresh cooked potatoes are king over potato chips. So why bring potato chips into your home? Rather let them indulge by putting a lot of butter on a hot potato and making a treat of it.

Most publications that talk about health and eating don't take into account your problems at home. It's true that someone whose health is not up to par will suddenly force himself to eat what's good for him. Or some adults will eat right because they should and want to feel good. But, your kids and even some adult members in your family will give you a hard time for your efforts.

193

I have used a lot of ways to get my gang to eat good things. Most of the time they didn't realize it. Of course, both Alton and I stress good eating habits all around at home and make them take a little of everything on the table even if it's only a teaspoonful. As a result, our kids eat almost everything.

In the next pages is an idea exchange. Most of these are mine, but if you like this sort of thing and have good or better ones, send them to me and I'll put them together into another book next year along with more of mine.

• I want to tell you about a goof that happened to me, where I knew it could happen and forgot it. We had company and I made instant gelatin (Page 70) using 2 tablespoons of gelatin and a can of frozen grape juice and a can of frozen pineapple juice. Well, I turned it out of the blender a nice fluffed, thick mass of gelatin. I cut a banana into it and set it on the counter ready to serve. When I was ready to serve it, part of it was liquid and I had the embarrassing pleasure of watching the whole thing turn to juice before our eyes. The reason was the pineapple juice. Frozen pineapple juice is raw and raw pineapple has an enzyme that attacks the protein in gelatin and breaks it down.

• *Party Mix*—Mix up a good combination of bite sized seeds and nuts such as mixed nuts, pumpkin seeds, sunflower seeds, and divide in half. Add whole soybeans and raw peanuts to one half and roast all together. When almost done, add unsweetened coconut and finish all together. Add the half of raw seeds that were left and flavor with vegetable or your favorite seasoning. Soybeans and peanuts cannot be eaten raw. Soybeans are hard but it seems kids like them. The roasting temperature should be about 350°. The chewable acerola tablets are good chewed with a mix like this and add a pretty pink color.

194

• Got leftover pancake or waffle batter? Pour it into a buttered pan and bake. Frost with a mixture of honey and peanut butter mixed well. This is good bread for dinner. Good on corn bread and other quick breads too!

• Lay out number of eggs needed in a recipe before you start breaking them. If something should distract you, you won't forget how many are left to go.

To Scramble Fat-Free Eggs

• Break eggs into ¼ or ½ cup boiling water in pan. Scramble and stir continuously until they go together and cook into scrambled eggs. Light and fluffy.

• When using water to grate any vegetable in the blender always repeat using it and save the water for a place in soup, gravy or a drink, etc., to save the nutrition from the vegetables.

• In making cakes from recipes in Part I, use a *very full heaping* cup of unsifted flour.

• A little molasses is tasty added to honey and peanut butter for a spread.

• Spread thawed frozen raspberries or strawberries on banana cake and let the juice soak in either on the whole cake or on individual servings. This is a good flavor combination, and attractive.

• A simple cheese spread: Put an amount of melted butter in blender. Add cottage cheese until thick and smooth, helping along on the top. Spread on bun or piece of quick bread and broil a few minutes under broiler. Add instant soups for different flavorings.

195

• Easy fish fillet coatings: Plain—use brown rice flour, rice polishings or soybean flour. Soybean flour browns easily. For special fish coating that takes a little more time, have the fish fresh or defrosted. Dip in beaten egg (beat it fast in the blender), then dip in brown rice flour and coat well. Brown in hot oil.

• For a different way to fix fish fillets, broil them under the broiler. Most fish are done by broiling on one side. If they are done they will fall apart when turned over. When cooked, spread one of the mayonnaises in this book on the fish thick. Broil until brown and serve.

• Brown rice can be cooked either by starting it in cold water, or by having the water boiling first. Brown rice cooked with 3 parts of water to one part of rice, started on a high heat and then turned down to low heat until the rice has absorbed all the water, will be white and fluffy like white rice.

• Don't throw away the tough part of an asparagus stalk. Cut it off where it's tender. Use the tender tops for cooking and put the tough part in the blender with water or favorite juice, and chop and strain for use in a fresh salad. Use the water in with an iced juice drink and really make use of that asparagus!

• Have to make a meal in a hurry and no meat defrosted? Put frozen hamburger in the kettle with a little water. Let it cook, covered, and once in a while scrape off the defrosted meat. When it's all pretty well defrosted and crumbled, add onion (if you like it) and sprinkle basil all over it. Let it steam on low. This is real good served on rice or with potatoes.

• Glass jars insure long storage life for your seeds, grains and flours. If covered tightly, they keep out insects and even mice. Sometimes the nicest homes will find a mouse in the cellar. Grain seeds kept in jars have a long storage life. The exception is pumpkin and sunflower seeds. They do become rancid after a long period, unless they are in the freezer. The reason for this could be that the outer covering is removed from them.

• School or other box lunches can be planned into the previous day's evening dinner or supper. A few extra potatoes cooked can be made into salad by adding mayonnaise, a little onion, pickle pieces, celery, pimento, parsley or whatever you like, the next morning. Most meats are good cold if dolled up a little, sliced and seasoned a bit. Rice is good mixed with fruit and sweet dressing (Pages 119 and 120). Just use your imagination and cook for both at once! Baby food jars and any small jars are good for packing good leftovers for box lunches.

• There seems to be a difference in the quality of carob powder. I find that with some batches I have bought, I had to add more to get the desired flavor. Some of it seems to have a grainier texture on the tongue when used in milk shakes, for example.

• Your favorite recipes for marinades for steak are perfect blended in a blender.

• A simple instant spice vinegar for flavoring salad dressings, relishes, etc., is to blend ½ cup vinegar, ½ cup of honey, ⅓ cup of mixed pickling spices. Blend a long time and strain through fine strainer. Keep refrigerated. Add only a few drops as it doesn't take much. Watch the red peppers in the spice mix and don't let too many fall in. This can be cooked too and strained, but it becomes a spice syrup then.

197

• Three tasty salad dressings: Basic Honey Mayonnaise, Page 117, and Tomato Garlic Dressing, Page 112. Then mix equal parts of each for another tasty French-type dressing with a flavor all its own.

• Onions, Egyptian or any kind, can be chopped with oil first in the blender, then transferred into the skillet for frying or sauteing meats such as liver and onions, etc.

• Liquid vitamin C from any health catalogue is good added to any juice drink. Also adds good flavor to teas. Also good on fruit as mentioned under fruit salads.

• A gargle that I read about and found to be good for a bad cough or throat is vinegar and honey in a little water—the stronger the better. Add some liquid vitamin C to it, gargle and then swallow it. Any liquid vitamin is good for this or one containing more than just vitamin C.

• From *Let's Live* magazine an article about one family's handed-down remedy for wounds or bad bruises: Grate a fresh carrot (preferably a home grown organic one) and apply as a poultice to the wound. There's no scientific basis for this, only experience that it works. She writes that she learned this from her husband's family. She also stated that it hurts more for a short while and then the pain lets up. We tried it once and it did seem to work. Tie the grated carrots on with a clean cloth and change, using fresh grated carrots if needed. Our Lane Alton got his finger smashed in something after I read this so I tied some grated carrots on and he was pleased with the relief.

• Have you tried papaya juice? This is a delicious drink and good for digestion. It seems to be highly recommended everywhere as a tasty addition to punch, milk shakes and drinks. I like to use it to make a drink out of the water used to chop vegetables in the blender. Also makes good gelatins.

• About chopping cold meat for these special sandwich spreads and perhaps for canapes: These are something I just haven't made too much of, but have a lot of questions on when I'm demonstrating blenders. I've tried all varieties of cold meats and cold roasts, chicken or home cooked meats. They all chop real well in any blender. You might have to push it down on the sides or stop the blender once in a while to push it into the blades. Chop about 1 cupful at a time, either cubed or in chunks. Mix with mayonnaise to taste. Add finely diced onion, pickle relish, and maybe pimento for color. Chopped cooked egg is good in this too.

• To add cooked, chopped egg to a recipe like a sandwich spread or potato salad, you don't have to go through the work of cooking eggs in the shell. Break them into a hot skillet in a little water, butter or oil, and scramble them while they cook and add to the salad.

• Having an assortment of different molds for gelatins can be a stimulus for children to eat. Gelatin puddings or fruit gelatins are good for them, and you can be a little sneaky here on what you blend into some of them. If served in a plain bowl, they might ask, "what's all in this?" But served up fancy in molds takes their minds to the looks of it more than the "ins" of it.

• Putting a chili or spaghetti sauce in the blender thickens and smooths it and cuts down cooking time.

• I grind white sugar into powdered sugar when demonstrating blenders to show the ability of that blender. Not all blenders do as good a job at this, however. It was here that one of the customers said that the frostings are so much sweeter when made with blender powdered sugar. Then a man overhearing this told me that he had a relative working in a sugar plant and that cornstarch is added to the powdered sugar before it is packed. He said anyone can observe this on a tour through the plant. So I learned something I didn't know before.

• I believe smell is more important than timing in cooking. This can be developed so that you can tell by the smell in your kitchen that a cake is done, or that meat, etc., is the way you like it. Timing can be misleading because directions have to be followed so exactly. Meat has to be so many pounds, and defrosted completely, cake pans exactly the size called for, etc. If you want to be a real cook, a sixth sense has to be developed on your own. Then you can have success regardless of what you are working with. Of course the two can be put together and used.

• Adding peppermint extract to sunflower seeds in a covered jar and letting them absorb it, makes a tasty novelty for a chewy snack. Vanilla is good too. I have seen vanilla beans for sale in the supermarket, but didn't buy any because they were so expensive. But I bet that would be good put into a jar of seeds.

• A simple effective way to rid your kitchen of so-called fruit or vinegar flies! Just put an overripe banana or anything that you see they like real well into the oven. Leave it ajar overnight and put away all fruit or attractions for them into a tight place so they can't get at anything else. In the morning close the door quickly and turn the oven on to about 200 degrees for a while. Repeat as often as necessary. If you have them in a cellar or storage room, you can use an electric pan or electric roaster, putting some goodies in for them and leaving the lid slightly ajar, so they think that they are sneaking in on something. But don't lift the lid to see how many there are because too many leave in a hurry. Close the lid fast and turn on the heat. This works well for me. Another way is to use the same method, only carry the container outside after you close it up and release them out of the house. If you catch them in a bag or empty oatmeal box with a small hole on top, close the hole and burn them in the incinerator.

• A blender will sometimes get stuck on something like a piece of carrot. When turning it on, if throwing it into high doesn't get it pulled through, you'll just have to stop and work it out with a knife.

• I have found soybean flour good for coating spring chicken before browning it. Oat flour also browns beautifully when used on spring chickens and fryers.

• Potatoes cut into wedges or pieces for browning in oil seem to have a better flavor and brown nicer than the usual slicing.

• For restaurant-type steaks and hamburgers, try pan broiling. Have a flat bottomed fry pan hot when you drop the steaks or hamburgers in; cover it and turn the heat to medium. Keep the meat simmering without juicing. If you see that the heat has gotten low enough to allow the meat to start juicing, turn it up. After a while you can tell by the sound if the heat needs turning up or down. Slash the steak on the sides to keep the meat from curling. Only sirloin, rib, T-bone, or tenderized steak is tender enough to be used for broiling. Don't season the meat until it's removed to the platter because seasoning ahead causes it to juice.

• Eggs, cooked, scrambled, or fried, that were left over at breakfast can be worked into other dishes during the day—such as potato, tuna, or any salad, or into any of my instant pudding recipes.

• Fresh green or yellow snap beans from the garden should never be washed before cleaning. It will almost double the time it takes you to clean them. Once they are wet everything hangs to them as a magnet. Snap off the stem end and rub them off while they are dry with your fingers, then wash them. Beans that are mulched are usually very clean.

• Mashed potatoes are easily made from potatoes that were cooked with skins, if you own a ricer. When they are cooked soft, throw into ricer and rice. The peelings are held back and you need only stir the riced potatoes with a spoon and add what you add: butter, milk, etc., and it's done!

• *Orange Jelly Roll*—Spread a can of frozen orange juice on a jelly roll and roll up. Something good and different. (Jelly Roll on Page 28.)

• Frozen pineapple juice makes a good steak tenderizer and marinade. The enzymes go to work on the meat the same as papaya does. Add onion and the seasonings that you like.

• *Easy Fudge Candy*—2 tablespoons each of carob, raw sugar, peanut oil. Add 1 teaspoon vanilla and 1 egg yolk. Stir together and beat like mad. Form into a roll and cut up.

• *Date Sweets (From Selma Long, Cashion, Okla.)*

In blender:
  2 eggs
  3 cups date crunches soaked in 1 cup hot water

In bowl:

> 2 cups oatmeal flour (either oat flour or oatmeal ground in blender)
> 1 tablespoon baking powder
> 1 teaspoon cinnamon
> 1½ teaspoons nutmeg
> ½ cup black walnuts in pieces
> 1 cup oil

Date crunches are not regular dates, but available from Califruit, Calimesa, California.

• *Dippity Doop*—I learned something from my aunt, Mrs. Melitta Huber, that I didn't know before. That is, that women used to cook flax seed for making wave set. I fooled around with this knowing from cereals how thick flax will get after it's moist. If you don't want to bother cooking it, it will get thick if you do nothing more than put ¾ cup of flax seeds into 2 cups of water. Let stand several hours and it gets thick by itself, stirring now and then. The seeds will settle and the goop can be poured off the top. You'll find the seeds starting to sprout and are delicious chewing, just for the fun of it. I think flax seeds are good to chew on anyway. As for a hair set, it gives the hair a nice soft body.

• *Bread Crumbs*—Do you use bread crumbs in your cooking? The easiest way to make them is to wad up a piece of bread *before* it's dried out, as hard as you can and throw the bread wad in the blender and it will chop like magic. This works on *all* blenders. If your blender doesn't grab the bread wad, just push it into the blades before you turn the blender on. These bread crumbs dry very fast and they can be stored.

• Perhaps the best way to cook soybeans is just to cover them with water, cook on a low heat until they are soft, and serve right away with butter and seasonings to taste. They have a tendency to get chewy when used in baked beans—although they are tasty. They harden up after they cool. Cooked soybeans are good added to chili soup either all soybeans or as part of the beans. Cooking them in the pressure cooker results in faster cooking, but does not soften them to a greater degree. They also will harden some after they cool. By this I mean, they will still be soft, but chewy.

• Tomatoes don't have to be canned if you are short of time. They are just as good frozen any way in the freezer—whole, cut up or whatever. Freeze them without peeling. The peeling zips right off under hot running water. Those that you cut up, you can use for blending for sauces and dressings and the peeling can be strained out through a wire strainer. Keep a jar thawing in the refrigerator and you'll always have some ready to use.

• Pumpkin peeled, can be used in much the same way as carrots. You can grate it into salads and use it raw anywhere you use carrots, including some in blender drinks. The pumpkin seeds can be dried and eaten, taking the seed out of the shells between your teeth, like a parrot does, or if you are watching T.V. take them out with a sharp knife while you sit.

• Have you tried rye flour? It is really good and makes delicious products. I never realized this, being scared of it from the unusual taste of commercial rye bread and also the same taste in the supermarket rye flour. But when I was misunderstood and got 25 pounds of rye flour instead of rice flour in one of my orders from the miller, I had to start using it and found out how tasty it is. Getting it freshly ground without any sifting makes all the difference in the world. Try it sometime: It makes good quick breads, cookies, or anything.

• *Yummy Rye Muffins*—Blend 1 cup milk (any kind), 3 eggs, ½ cup oil. Pour over 1¾ cup unsifted rye flour

with 1 tablespoon baking powder mixed in. Add a cupful of loose raisins, a handful of nutmeats and a tablespoon of cinnamon and stir. Bake at 350° until done in
buttered muffin tins. Makes 18. Serve with butter and
honey while still warm if possible.

• I think one of the best pieces of literature I have ever
read on sensible natural eating was sent to me by Dr.
William A. Ellis of Tarentum, Pa. This is a reprint of a
speech given by him from a doctor's viewpoint of seeing
and treating actual people. No fads or cultist ideas here,
just the best ever, easy-to-understand explanation on
eating and its cause and effects. One especially important aspect of this speech is his easy-to-understand out-
line leading into stomach acidity and alkalinity which
can cause death and be misdiagnosed as a heart attack.
A simple test is to drink a little apple cider vinegar in
water. If that relieves the chest pains it was nothing
more than an over alkaline stomach, which is the more
common the older we get. This is contrary to the T.V.
commercials he says, that would have us believe we are
all over-acid. So try this if you overeat or have burning
or chest pains. I felt it is something we all should know.
Soda and antacids only make the condition worse.

I don't know if he sells this reprint. It is 11 pages
long and as I said, one of the best and most sensible I
have ever read. The title is "Are We Eating A Diseased
Diet?"

From Ilona Parker, Messena, N.Y.
• She writes, "For years I've had some liver powder
here and didn't know what to do with it. It didn't seem
to go well with anything. Now I find to my amazement
that liver powder dissolves very well with your carob
pudding. I think I have put as many as 8 tablets into the
pudding and it is not noticeable."

All of us know what a good food liver is and all of us
know very few like it. Here is a splendid way to add it

to a meal if you need to or want to. (Carob Smooth Pudding, Page 87.)

She also writes me that the Millyun Dollar Mix (Page 22) seems to turn out better than regular flour when she uses it in place of regular flour in her own recipes, including pie crust made from the recipe on the Planter's Peanut Oil bottle.

She also writes about something which we have done many times, but I forgot to print it and I want to thank her for reminding me. The Carob Pudding (Page 87) makes delicious frozen fudgesickles. I bought some fudgesickle forms years ago, and whenever I make pudding, the kids like to freeze themselves fudgesickles. Any of the dairyless or other puddings in this book work well for this.

• *Banana Fudgesickles*

Now, here's an idea of hers that sounds like a real kids' pleaser. She cuts bananas crosswise into three or four pieces. Put a wooden stick or a holder in each end and freeze. When frozen dip into the Carob Pudding and return to freezer.

These are the kinds of letters that I like to get. We mothers are supposed to be smarter than our children (at least for a few years) and with a little ingenuity we can work it so they eat anything we want them to, instead of throwing our hands up and complaining that the kids just won't eat.

• *Thick Mayonnaise and oils (From Daisie Weaver, Stehekin, Wash.)*

Daisie read in *Wheat And Sugar Free* about the trouble I've had with some oils not thickening in the blender when making mayonnaise, and when changing bottles, even with the same brand, it will thicken. Well this is still happening to me. Some bottles of oil just won't thicken including cold pressed oils. Anyway this is what she wrote:

"I thought you might like to know what I do with a batch of mayonnaise that won't thicken. I have had the same trouble, only mostly with safflower oil. So now I always use corn oil to start the mayonnaise. After I get a good emulsion, I can add any kind of oil for the quantity I want to make. But if I have a batch that does not thicken nice and stiff, I just add it slowly to a thickened batch, and it always turns out OK. I just do not know what makes one batch turn out OK and another will not."

Now I've done this too since she wrote me, added a thin batch to a thick batch and all does thicken. It seems cold pressed corn oil will thicken every time but not commercial brands. Safflower oil and soybean oil are unpredictable. Peanut oil always has thickened for me, supermarket brand or cold pressed. Supermarket brands of peanut oil give off an oilier taste or flavor that cold pressed peanut oil doesn't seem to have. Soybean oil has a different taste although not unpleasant. Corn oil is one of the mildest flavored oils. Sunflower oil has a flavor on the stronger oilier side. I've found that the cold pressed oils are the mildest and none are so strong that vanilla or flavoring in a recipe can't take care of it.

PECANS

In the September 1966 issue of *Natural Food and Farming* there was an article by John M. Ellis, M.D., about vitamin B6 deficiency. I know I can't do justice to this article in trying to condense it but the symptoms of this deficiency are so much like the complaints of people around us. To make it short, it causes a neuritis type of stiffness in the shoulders, such as waking up with a stiff aching arm, numbness and tingling in fingers and hands and on to edema with swelling, which is especially true for women, which causes leg cramps etc. As it gets worse, pain in the pectoral region of the chest radiates through the arms and shoulders, and hands become crippled. Also a puffiness and sheen of the skin is noticed. This is true of both men and women. Anyway, Doctor Ellis treated this with Vitamin B6 by mouth and some of the more severe cases with B6 shots, with success.

Then a year later in the September 1967 issue, of the same magazine, Doctor Ellis has narrowed this treatment down to a food, namely pecans. I will reprint some of his writing here. But please do take into account one thing as you read it; it means working *raw* pecans into your diet, not baking them into cookies, candies, cakes, etc., and still thinking you are doing something good. This is where the blender shines, even if you have family members who don't like raw nuts. They can be thrown into almost anything you make in the blender unnoticed. You can add them to milk shakes, ice cream, blender drinks, salads, puddings or almost any blender recipe in these two books that don't require cooking. They are very good added to cereal or even salad dressings. If everyone does like nuts and you add them, add them last and only let them chop coarse so they can be chewed and enjoyed.

The following is a part of the September 1967 article which *Natural Food and Farming* gave me permission to reprint.

THE ROLE OF THE PECAN IN THE DIET

by John M. Ellis M.D.

Author of *The Doctor Who Looked At Hands*

It was six years ago that I became intensely interested in human nutrition, and surprising as it may seem to some, pecans have led me to some findings that must surely be of far reaching significance. Perhaps it should be mentioned, however, that most doctors of medicine find themselves in one of two opposing camps. They either believe that our people are in a state of excellent nutrition, or they believe that thousands of our people are suffering from latent and marginal degenerative diseases that arise from malnutrition. It has been my usual fortune, for the first time of any, to observe through dietary change, improvement of signs and symptoms of diseases that have puzzled doctors and plagued the civilized world for centuries. It would be of interest to you to know that by giving my patients in Northeast Texas twelve raw pecans daily, I learned that a form of painful neuritis and arthritis of shoulders, arms, and hands could be relieved in six weeks. It would be of interest to know that I have observed patients who ate twelve raw pecans daily for as long as a year.

Eventually, I learned, through a process of elimination, that I could effect these same improvements with a tremendously important, but infrequently thought of, vitamin, namely—*pyridoxine* or *Vitamin B6*. On the 30th anniversary of the discovery of Vitamin B6, there was held in New York, an international symposium, at which scientists from many nations discussed for three days the research that has been done relative to Vitamin B6. And in pecans, man has one of his richest natural sources of Vitamin B6, and in a form that is not only edible, but appetizing.

There is one very important scientific fact that might unlock fortunes for pecan growers. Vitamin B6 is destroyed by 245° heat. This has been proven by many scientists, and it is important to realize that pecans can be eaten raw and without being cooked or heated. Other foods, such as meat, are rich in Vitamin B6, but who can eat raw meat? The wheat kernel has Vitamin B6, but who eats raw wheat? And then there is brewers yeast with its rich store of vitamins, but who finds raw yeast appetizing? Again and again we can return to pecans because they can be eaten raw and with pleasure, and in sufficient quantity to be effective.

Now, how much Vitamin B6 is in a pecan? Frankly, I doubt if anyone knows exactly. Scientists who have worked with the subject for years have had difficulty in assaying B6 in foods. But enough has been learned to know that all of the tree nuts are rich in Vitamin B6. Proper conception of this might well mean that all of the tree nuts are among our most precious foods.

It has been proven that over 30 enzymatic reactions in the human body depend on Vitamin B6 and it is now known that Vitamin B6 must be present in adequate and substantial amounts for metabolism of proteins in muscles, nerves, and even the brain of the human body. There is indication that mental retardation is a result of Vitamin B6 deficiency. Extensive animal research has shown that monkeys developed hardening of the arteries when they were placed on Vitamin B6 deficient diets, and I have seen photographs of the teeth of those monkeys and decay had progressed to the point that the teeth appeared as if they had been knocked out with hammers, whereas control monkeys did not exhibit such tooth decay.

In a more general consideration of pecans in the human diet, it should be mentioned that pecans are rich in other B vitamins, pecans are rich in polyunsaturated fats, and pecans are rich in calories. It would appear to me that when any product is sold, it should be sold on its longest and strongest points, after scientific investigations, and to people who need and want the product because of its merits. Obese and overly fat people do not need and should not have the high energy of pecans, but there are millions of people in this and other countries who *do* need the rich store of calories in pecans, and all people need the vitamins in pecans. Since the B vitamins cannot be stored in the body, they must be eaten daily in sufficient quantity. With regard to polyunsaturated fats, it should be mentioned that these fats have less hydrogen in the molecules and it has been found that the polyunsaturated fats are more completely metabolized by the human body as compared to the saturated or animal fats which have more hydrogen in the molecules. Many scientists in many countries have done thousands of experiments which in some way link excessive use of animal fats with hardening of the arteries and heart disease. Many scientists are in agreement that there is a natural hand in glove reaction between Vitamin B6 and certain of the polyunsaturated fats. Pecans are rich in both Vitamin B6 and polyunsaturated fats.

CONCLUSION

My sincerest thanks to all who bought *Wheat And Sugar Free*! If it were not for all the letters that I have received, I never would have undertaken writing *Blenderbusz*.

This book is by no means a complete book on using the blender, but I hope to have started you on an easier and quicker method of cooking. It is a modern approach on cooking from scratch. If you have no desire to give in to cooking from mixes but still are short on time, I'm sure you can use many ideas in here and at the same time use products that are wholesome and nutritious. It is possible to make foods with natural products that can compete in taste and appeal with any you can buy on the market.

Four years ago we went to the World's Fair in New York. We pulled a camper trailer and stayed overnight in trailer camps. One fact present everywhere along the line was the way everybody trusted one another. There were camping equipment and valuables in sight everywhere. In mentioning this to somebody, they told us people that camp seem to be a certain quality of people. Nothing ever seems to get stolen.

I feel I can say the same thing about people interested in their health and welfare. They are a certain quality of people. I wish I could share the thoughts and humor of the letters I received. Some of the letters were from very elderly folks whose writing or typing and spirits show that they are very young indeed. This fact I also notice when I demonstrate. The people that stop and are interested are a certain type of people. They have that something about them, neat and well dressed and alert looking. Once in a while someone turns up his nose at what I am showing and it always turns out to be a type of person that looks sick and has a bad skin and color. This has run so true to form that it's almost possible to tell by the looks of a person if I can interest him or not in owning a blender.

It is too bad that there are some people that talk health and good living but don't practice it. This is what gives things the label of being a so-called fad and spoils what is really a truly good thing.

What are my qualifications for writing a cookbook? None. I am not a home economics major. In fact, I took home economics one year in high school and hated it. I'd probably feel different about it now though. Experience was the teacher.

If I print another book, it will be with your help. There are some requests for recipes that I'm still working on and haven't gotten worked out satisfactorily yet. You might have to hide this and the next one if we don't want our benefactors to find out what we are all up to. Isn't this underground cooking fun?

INDEX

215

216

223

224

NEW BOOKS BY THE MOST POPULAR
AUTHORS IN THE HEALTH FIELD

How Many Have You Read?

☐ **BE SLIM AND HEALTHY** by Linda Clark. An original book. Shows you how to have a trimmer body the natural way. Includes a unique **Stop and Go Carbohydrate Computer.** ($1.25)

☐ **GO AHEAD AND LIVE** by Mildred Loomis. An expert on youth problems offers practical advice on coping with today's challenges. Never before in paperback. (95¢)

☑ **FACE IMPROVEMENT THROUGH DIET AND EXERCISE** by Linda Clark. An original book demonstrating—with text and drawings—a sane, healthful way to facial loveliness. (95¢)

☑ **FACT/BOOK ON YOGURT AND KEFIR** by Beatrice Trum Hunter. An original book with many, many recipes by the author of **The Natural Foods Cookbook.** (95¢)

☐ **MY SECRETS OF NATURAL BEAUTY** by Virginia Castleton Thomas. By the beauty editor of **Prevention** Magazine— recipes for cosmetics; exercises; organic facial treatments;— a treasure trove of help for teenagers, women in the middle years and those over fifty. Never before in print. Quality paperback edition $2.95. Clothbound $5.95

Buy them at your local bookstore or use this handy coupon

Keats Publishing, Inc., Dept. M3
212 Elm St., New Canaan, Conn. 06840

Please send me the books checked above. I am enclosing $_____. (Check or money order—no currency, no C.O.D.'s, please. If less than 4 books, add 10¢ per book for postage and handling. We pay postage on 4 books or more.) Please allow up to three weeks for delivery.

Name_____

Address_____

City_____State_____Zip_____